Praise
for
Fear and Loathing of Boca Raton

"Leave it to the author of *Zen and the Art of Fatherhood* to show us that the Tao is not to be found in Taos, that Ken Kesey's bus "Further" was no RV, that "far out" is not necessarily far away, and that dropping out doesn't have to mean dropping everything we love for some white-belted, pastel-colored gated community of eternal golf. Just when I thought that the sixties were really over—'Holy flashback, Batman, they're back!'"

—Gary Allen, food writer and author of *The Herbalist in the Kitchen*

"While I'm impressed to see Steven Lewis can function as a sexagenarian father of seven after enduring the drug abuse of the 1960s, I'm even more impressed at this impassioned and hilarious look at entering the dreaded senior years. His determination to hold onto a youthful spirit and keep the tides of geriatric-hood at bay brings to mind another 60-year-old fighter, Winston Churchill, who vowed to 'fight on the fields and in the streets...fight in the hills; we shall never surrender.'"

—Jacob Lewis, managing editor, *The New Yorker*

"With humor, care, and an overriding desire to tell the truth, Lewis reminds us of who we are no matter what our age, brand identification, musical preference or family history. This is a book for all generations, because the one it describes is not what it is anymore or what it would have been anyway—and somehow, with a gracious smile of recognition, of how good it never was. This book takes the fear out of tomorrow because it sees today as it is, and yesterday as it never was to so many. Those who see themselves in this book are capable of peace. Those who do not are unable to experience grace. All will laugh with knowledge."

—Dr. Martin Jack Rosenblum, historian emeritus, Harley-Davidson Motor Company; author of *Searching For Rock And Roll; Harley-Davidson Lore, Volumes I and II; Harley-Davidson Motor Company: 1903–1993; The Holy Ranger: Harley-Davidson Poems.*

"Don't take the brown antacid! *Fear and Loathing of Boca Raton* is the best Rx for the gray-ponytail set since the universal legalization of marijuana (in my dreams). If you can imagine Neal Cassady behind the wheel of a Winnebago, stopping to pick up a hitchhiking Herman Hesse en route to a retirement community, then you've got the tone of this genial, freewheeling, and yet refreshingly skeptical set of riffs on the 1960s and their various aftermaths—including the care and feeding of the next generation and the refusal to be burnt out while continuing to celebrate peace, love, and other endangered but incorruptible hippie values."

—Mikhail Horowitz, former cultural czar, *Woodstock Times*, author of *Big League Poets*

"*Fear and Loathing in Boca Raton* is a road map through the awkward conversion from war-protesting, LSD-taking youth to the acceptance (and rejection) of retirement communities and pleather footwear. Lewis is, as always, insightful and hilarious and knows this subject deep in his heart. His take on the predicament he (and all children of the 60s) faces will keep you turning pages."

—Kate Lewis, managing editor, *SELF Magazine*

"Put on your best green party pants and Members Only jacket and climb aboard Lewis's Deadhead sticker-sporting Cadillac SUV. Enjoy the long, strange trip alongside Sal Paradise, Lou Reed, and Bill Borroughs as Lewis brilliantly navigates us on a southbound route from Woodstock to Assisted Living. Boca Raton looming brightly like a bug zapper in the distance. Lewis's funny, sharp, insightful observations will get you there just in time for the early-bird special. To paraphrase the Maharishi Mahesh Yogi, 'Don't just do something, sit there. And while you're at it, read this terrific book!'"

—Peter Steinfeld, screenwriter, *Echo, Drowning Mona, Analyze That, Be Cool*

"Steve Lewis came of age in the era of free love, LSD, and rock and roll. His brilliant new book, *Fear and Loathing of Boca Raton: A Hippies Guide to the Second Sixties* is a manifesto for former flower children about staying hip and relevant. Forget the early-bird special. Slip into a tie-dyed T-shirt, down a shot of warm milk and your favorite antidepressant, and take one cool Kama Sutra ride toward the new Strawberry Fields."

—Kathyrn Gurfein, The Kathryn Gurfein Writing Fellowship at Sarah
     Lawrence College

Fear and Loathing of Boca Raton

A Hippies' Guide to the *Second* Sixties

by
Steven Lewis

For Cindy and Marty, with best wishes and thanks for the gracious invitation to the East Fishkill Community Library, Steven Lewis

Quill Driver Books

Sanger, California

Printed in the United States of America.

Published by
Quill Driver Books/Word Dancer Press, Inc.,
1254 Commerce Ave, Sanger, CA 93657
559-876-2170 / 800-497-4909
QuillDriverBooks.com

Quill Driver Books/Word Dancer Press books may be purchased for educational, fund-raising, business or promotional use. Please contact Special Markets, Quill Driver Books/Word Dancer Press, Inc. at the above address or phone numbers.

Quill Driver Books/Word Dancer Press Project Cadre:
David Marion, Stephen Blake Mettee, Carlos Olivas, Cassandra Williams

First Printing

ISBN 1-884956-74-2 • 978-1884956-74-4

**To order a copy of this book, please call
1-800-497-4909.**

Library of Congress Cataloging-in-Publication Data
Lewis, Steven M.
Fear and loathing of Boca Raton : a hippies' guide to the second sixties / by
Steven Lewis.
p. cm.
ISBN-13: 978-1-884956-74-4 (trade pbk.)
ISBN-10: 1-884956-74-2 (trade pbk.)
1. Hippies—Life skills guides. 2. Counterculture—Handbooks, manuals, etc. 3.
Aging—Handbooks, manuals, etc. I. Title.
HM647.L48 2007
305.260973—dc22
2007031469

For Patti, You're Still the One

For Bruce Schenker, Eternal Hipster and Friend

For Clay, Devin, Bella, Rory, Connor, Maddie, Schuyler, Jack, Charlee, Eleanor…and all those beautiful Aquarian babies to follow

Take a load off, Fanny
from *"The Weight"* by The Band

Versions of the following titles originally appeared in:

Pulse Magazine, "Deadhead Driver in a Cadillac" (Intro)
Christian Science Monitor, "And a Note About Combovers" (Chapter Four)
Dutchess Magazine, "Being and Healthiness" (Chapter Five) and "To 'too or Not to 'too" (Chapter Twenty-One)
New Paltz Times, "Lost in the Health Care Bureaucracy" (Chapter Six) and "Choosing a Handle …" (Chapter Fourteen)
The New York Times, "Empty Nest: Take Two" (Chapter Nineteen)
AARP, "My Resignation from the Old Men's Club" (Chapter Twenty-Two)

Contents

Acknowledgments

*M*any, many, many thanks to Isabel Burton and Violet Gaynor for their sophisticated, wry, witty fashion contributions to this good book; to Bill and Jack Sheeley, ace pharmacists, for their patient and helpful advice on post-sixty uppers and downers; to Dr. Marj Steinfeld and Dr. Cynthia Pizzulli for their psychological insight on relationships; to Debra Morrison and Ruth Hayden for valuable perspectives on money matters; to Andrew Kossover and Arlene Dubin for their astute legal counsel; to Doc Rock for letting me use his Woodstock song list; to Gary Allen, Linda Drollinger, Larry Feldman, Irene Berner, and Beverly Wallace for sharing their glorious memories of Woodstock; to Don Poss, Deanna Shlee Hopkins the late Adam Holloman, the late Mike Powell, Owen Luck, and Larry Winters for letting me use such haunting memories of Vietnam; to Michelle Diana and her 9th and 10th grade students at New Paltz High School (Marissa Barrington, Bridget Kelly, Dan Rudden, Ben Ruaric, Ksenia Ko Novalov, Jacob Crist, John Stephonson, Amanda Cora, Gabriella O'Shea, Danielle Salinitri, and Robin Caskey) for such invaluable advice on staying young at heart.

Appreciation after appreciation goes to the Millrock Writing Salon: Dahlia Bartz-Cabe, Mihai Grunfeld, Patricia Hunt-Perry, Tracy Leavitt, Ed McCann, Tom Nolan, Stephanie Padovani, and Larry and Helise Winters. And, because I have learned painfully well this past season how sustaining a little help from one's friends can be, endless gratitude goes to Richard Gaynor and Myron Adams, such selfless good pals.

Finally, I am remarkably grateful to the publisher of Quill Driver Books, Steve Mettee, who agreed to issue this book simply because he liked my writing. For an old hipster, that's just about as groovy as it gets.

Deadhead Driver
in a Cadillac

My father was born in Brooklyn in 1908; he later moved with his family to Hollis, Queens, and then, like so many kids from those immigrant streets, pushed, bulled, and bullied his way through the crowds and, as they said back then, made something out of himself.

The making did not come without cost, though. In the rubble of the Depression he gave up on his dream of being a lawyer (went to night school, passed the bar, but never practiced). And further down the same economic highway he came to that elemental fork: go left and be a model dad like Ward Cleaver; go right and doggedly pursue a career. So, six days a week my father left the house in Roslyn early every morning and came home long after the family had eaten dinner and had disappeared behind their hollow luan bedroom doors. Sundays, he did paperwork. Along the way my father missed out on every soccer, baseball, and basketball game I played at Wheatley High. Never made it to an awards assembly or a Cub Scout meeting. The man was so busy, so industrious, so single-minded in his pursuit of profit that when his eight-year-old son had collected enough Borden's ice cream cup lids to win a couple of bleacher seats for himself and his dad at Ebbets Field, my dad sent his warehouse manager Mortie in his place.

That said, the great sacrifices my old man made did not come without rewards. After years of putting an aching shoulder to the wheel on the Long Island Expressway, he was able to buy a small school supply business in Manhattan; and later a ranch house on suburban Candy Lane (yes, Candy Lane!) in Roslyn Heights. Then one day my father drove the solid, dependable Buick Roadmaster over to a dealer on Jericho Turnpike and traded up for his dream boat, a 1956, powder-blue Cadillac Coupe de Ville.

My dad stood next to that mile-long symbol of his success with a grin that was matched only in later years by the birth of his grandchildren. For what it's worth, his brothers, Murray (Hawaiian shirts) and Mac (plaid Bermuda shorts, argyle knee socks), who also made somethings of themselves, both drove Chrysler Imperials. Yet as soon as you saw that powder-blue beauty in the driveway, everyone knew that my old man had them beat.

When I reflect back on the great chasm that developed in the chasm-making sixties between many fathers and sons, I can't help but remember how I blamed the Cadillac for the rift that grew up between my father and me. In 1959, when he bought the second Caddy, the famous one with the big gaudy fins, our troubles were already beginning to appear like the pimples on my 13-year-old face. We soon tangled over everything. Everything. And by college—and Dylan—and Civil Rights—and long hair—and Vietnam—and a passing notion of Karma, I laid all my anger and frustration right at my father's garage on Candy Lane: I told him that when the revolution arrived there would be payback for him and his fellow suburban Caddy owners. He had no idea what I was talking about.

So in 1968, when I got married and he was just settling into Cadillac number four or five, I righteously vowed never to put money before family…or principle…or happiness. I would be a good dad. A great dad. Nothing would come before my children. If God Himself had pulled an Abraham on me, I would gladly submit to plague, pestilence, boils, and horrifying death before I sacrificed my child…before I missed one soccer game. And, of course, I would never to own a Cadillac.

So, you know where this is going…but let me drive you there on my route. I went on to lead the life I threatened him I would. I left Wisconsin (where I had spent ten years away from my father—going to college, getting married, teaching, becoming a father myself) and moved to the Shawangunk Mountains in upstate New York, where I went to every game, every concert, every ceremony, standing proudly next to my beautiful seven children just as he stood beaming beside his Cadillacs. And, from the driver's seat of a long succession of VW Vanagons and other clunky counter-culture cars, I scoffed along with Don Henley at all the businessmen with Deadhead stickers on their Cadillacs. I sneered at post-Hippie surgeons getting out of their Benz's to hang back at Dylan concerts. I guffawed when I saw Smith Barney traders with ponytails contorting themselves into their Boxsters. I drove a Honda full of stickers and dents and the spills and leakings of seven children and six grandchildren, until practically every warning light on the dashboard was lit— until the poor machine whined and grunted and practically begged me to put it down.

And then, as these things sometimes happen in the sometimes fortuitous circle of life, my wife got a call from her father who had recently bought a Cadillac SRX (the "small" SUV) and didn't like driving it. He offered it to us for a price that any responsible dad with bills to pay could not afford to turn down.

Thus, caught in the one-way traffic jam of my own making, I turned to my wife with a kneejerk "No! Just look at me…I'm a writer, a beach dog, a beatnik, a hippie.…I still have a VW bus in the barn! Cadillac owner, my ass!"

She looked at me like I was nuts. Just like my late father might have looked at me.

She was right, of course. So there I was all those incarnations later, Samuel Lewis' angry boy, all grown up (edging up on the big six-oh), and the reviled Caddy owner I had sworn never to become.

Please know that the SRX is a magnificent automobile. Please know, too, that I didn't have any illusions about the old man looking down—or up, as the case may be—gratified to know that the Prodigal Son had finally returned with some sense pounded into that thick skull. (If you must know, it would be a lock that he'd be grousing that I didn't wash and wax it.)

But in the first few months that I drove that lavish beast around this funky upstate town—and endured much teasing from friends and foes— I slowly gained a much deeper appreciation for my father's pleasures and the cosmic-sized sacrifices that went into attaining them…and, of course,

John Lennon's admonition about Instant Karma, which I played over and over on my six-disc CD changer.

My father may not have been a model dad like Ward Cleaver. But as that not-so-little gift from the universe taught me, I discovered that I was not a very good son…a James Joyce sized epiphany that blew mind and self-satisfied ego wide open. Mea culpa, mea culpa, mea maxima culpa.

However, if you are now assuming that since I made some sort of tenuous peace with my dad I'd be feeling a little mellower about Vietnam, Lyndon Johnson, Richard Nixon, Dow Chemical, Richard Daley, J. Edgar Hoover, the Bee Gees, Barry Preston, or Barry Goldwater, driving off into the sunset in my Cadillac SRX right into downtown Boca wearing my chartreuse party pants, red blazer, and white shoes, you'd have to be smoking the best Colombian on the street. Not me.

As soon as I was able to swing a deal, I dealt the Caddy for something I could drive around on the beach; something I could slide surfboards and plywood into and not worry about the Corinthian leather; something I could slap some bumper stickers on and not laugh at myself; something that takes me where I want to go.

That's what I hope this book does for you. This is not our parents' sixties.

Day One: Turn On, Tune In, Drop Out (Again)

Richie Havens
Minstrel From Gault
High Flyin' Bird
I Can't Make It Anymore
With A Little Help
Strawberry Fields For Ever
Hey Jude
I Had A Woman
Handsome Johnny
Freedom

Sweetwater
Motherless Child
Look Out
For Pete's Sake
Day Song
What's Wrong
Crystal Spider
Two Worlds
Why Oh Why

Bert Sommer
Jennifer
The Road To Travel
I Wondered Where You Be
She's Gone
Things Are Going My Way
And When It's Over
Jeanette

Tim Hardin
Misty Roses
If I Were A Carpenter

Ravi Shankar
Raga Puriya-Dhanashri/Gat In Sawarital
Tabla Solo In Jhaptal
Raga Manj Kmahaj/Alap Jor/Dhun In Kaharwa Tal/Medium & Fast Gat In Teental

Melanie
Beautiful People
Birthday Of The Sun

Arlo Guthrie
Coming Into Los Angeles
Walking Down The Line
Amazing Grace

Joan Baez
Joe Hill
Sweet Sir Galahad
Drug Store Truck Driving Man
Swing Low Sweet Chariot
We Shall Overcome

Chapter One

The Gray Album

Or, as the late great Dylan Thomas wrote shortly before he drank himself to death, "Do Not Go Gentle into that Good Night"

*W*ith apologies to the late great Lord Buckley and his classic Beatnik paean to Julius Caesar: "Hipsters, flipsters and finger poppin' daddies, knock me your lobes…, I have come to celebrate the sixties, not to bury us."

Rest assured there will be no wringing of my newly liver spotted hands, no bemoaning the crow's feet around my eyes or the creak in my knees. Nor will I take you on some kind of Peter Max-inspired sexagenarian acid trip of earthly delights awaiting all of us as soon as we jump on the mother ship. And, just in case you're wondering, I am decidedly not offering up the same establishment-driven drivel that crowds the shelves of our mega bookstores: *The Five (Seven-Ten-Twelve) Habits of Successful 60-Something CEOs Who Have Figured Out How To Avoid Aging and Death Through Offshore Investment…*or *The Five (Seven-Ten-Twelve) Gates to the Gloriously Transcendent and Marvelously Revisionist Golden Years.*

This book is what it is…a friendly extended riff on the cosmic—and not so cosmic—arithmetic of a generation, unlike any other generation, suddenly seeing the sixties through a brand-new and probably myopic set of eyes. In looking back over my shoulder I am powerfully aware that the age cannot be summed up by a Mason Williams compendium of images of Tim Leary, Mai Lai, Ram Dass, Ho Chi Minh, Jane Fonda, Martin Luther King, Andy Warhol, Roger Maris, Lyndon Baines Johnson, Maynard G. Krebs, the Velvet Underground, SDS, SNCC, LSMFT, the

Chicago Seven or the seven chakras, the Six Million Dollar Man, the Dave Clark Five, the Fab Four, the Three Stooges, the Two Towers, or the notion of Oneness as experienced through the holy trinity of sex, drugs, and rock and roll.

But it's all that as well.

And looking soberly ahead, way beyond the unholy trinity of Viagra, statins, and Wayne Newton in Vegas, I see vast opportunities for love and peace. I'm not pulling your leg.

Cut #1

Now that we have that out of the way, here are my assumptions about you, the eternal hipster behind those reading glasses:

• If you're checking out this book because it's not the only reading material in arm's reach from the toilet, it's most likely because you're about to climb Mount Sixty or already reached the peak some time ago.

• The ubiquitous AARP magazine has been arriving in your mailbox for a decade or more.

• As above, you haven't gotten around to reading the magazine yet.

• You've already been through the five stages of Senior Citizen Discounts: Repugnance, Denial, Irony, Temptation, and the Inevitable Surrender...the ahhhhhh of that first bittersweet lucre...10% off!

• You've been thinking about dropping out again—and this time for good.

• In your heart of hearts, you think the sixties were better in every way than the seventies, eighties, nineties, and the new millennium. And they probably were.

• You've had it up to here (imagine my hand above my head) with advice on health, longevity, retirement villages, active senior lifestyles, vaginal dryness, erectile dysfunction, peeing in the middle of the night, bowel movements.

• Some of you are beginning to think that it's okay to talk about your bowels in public. (It's not.)

• You don't want to be old—let's not kid ourselves, no one wants to be old—or, more reasonably, you don't want to act like an old fart.

• Above all, you don't want to be your parents.

And, in that last entry is the heart and soul of a generation of rebels—entering the great unknown without the stultifying baggage our parents carried into old age (at a remarkably young age now that I think about it).

This book is a celebration, a happening, if you will, a call to experience fully the everything that holds everything ahead of it.

But first, let me first go back to where it all began for me (me, because we were perhaps the first generation to understand that the specific foretells the general…and that the confessional voice is the one that truly grabs the listener's ear…or maybe it's just that I have your attention and it's my turn for show and tell).

Cut #2

All that is left of moving day 1951 for me is the memory of a curled black and white snapshot with scalloped edges. Not the actual 2 x 3 photograph itself, mind you. That's long gone. But from the eyes-closed image that remains, it's hard to tell which is more spindly, the bare maple tree that came with the brand-new ranch house or the skinny, big-eared four-and-a-half year old standing right next to it.

Fifty-six years later, with seven kids and now ten grandchildren riding my shoulders, I am by necessity not so spindly anymore. And, as I found on a recent sentimental journey downstate to the old quarter- acre homestead in Roslyn Heights, Long Island, NY, the spindly maple tree is gone. Nothing is left but a graphic off a TruGreen ChemLawn website: a weed-free carpet of flawless lawn right up to a perfect flagstone path, impeccable flower beds waiting for daffodils, manicured yew bushes, and a nondescript grey house that bears considerable resemblance to the one I grew up in.

We had moved from 135-18 77th Avenue in Kew Gardens to this potato farm bulldozed into a housing development in distant Nassau County. Despite the fact that it was a mere 13 miles from door-to-door, our old friends and family back in Queens and Brooklyn felt we had deserted them. They said we were moving to "the country."

A week before that elemental trek I had tripped on the concrete steps of our garden apartment building and howled like some spoiled brat in the peanut gallery on Howdy Doody. My Aunt Miriam, who would later courageously follow the wagon train across borough and county lines to her own plantation-sized quarter acre in wild and wooly Great Neck, soothed me by saying there'd be no steps at my brand new ranch house in the country.

Ranch house? I imagined a long, wooden, dusty front porch with Hoppy and Roy and Gabby and the rest of the boys twirling their six-shooters and clinking their spurs as they walked down the steps to organize the posse. Not quite.

Aunt Miriam was right about one thing, though. There were no sidewalks. Nor were the narrow roads in the development completely paved that February. In fact, we didn't even have phone service yet. The telephone company had to install a temporary booth down on the corner of Westwood Circle for emergency calls. So, this was true wilderness and we were settlers!

Most amazing to this undersized immigrant from the world of numbered avenues and honking traffic, the quiet road was named Candy Lane by some suburban visionary. That's right, Candy Lane. Did I think that candy canes would grow on that spindly tree, just like on the Candyland game board? Absolutely. Did I know that I would later spend my college days in mortal fear that anyone would find out that I grew up on Candy Lane? No.

Thus, the universe was full of possibility for me and all the other Baby Boomer kids who were to enter kindergarten the following fall at the I.U. Willets Road Elementary School. And, I suppose, for all those parents who courageously cut their own taproots so that their children would know the post-war bliss of crickets and barbeque grills and chartreuse dinette sets and two-car garages and pink mohair sweaters.

And, so a full 56 years after jumping out of the five-acre back seat of the loaded-down Hudson and hitting the terra-surfaced driveway of the quarter-acre tract house, my Candy Lane appeared more like a Lionel train set-up to me than a real street. Driving slowly past the Schnippers' barely recognizable renovated house, it was hard to believe that this now-chemicalized soil ever supported a potato farm, much less a spindly maple tree. Or that the original second generation Jewish settlers in this rural outpost of civilization, the Weils, the Danzigers, the Formans, the Diamonds—ever raised kids here. No one was on the street. No punchball, no marbles, no bikes tossed onto the lawns. No one working under the hood of a car. The great sense of renewal and possibility had been edited out of this scene. Everything was very neat, very settled, and very prosperous. And very dead.

In February 1951, however, with a light snow on the grassless ground along Candy Lane, everything was as bright and white for this boy and this country as the bulb that instantly lit when we opened the brand new GE refrigerator. Speaking for GE, the actor Ronald Reagan told us that "Progress is our most important product." And, we believed him.

Cut #3

What went wrong?

Well, something, everything. I suspect that all the myths and lies of the American Dream, "1950s version," caught up to the culture. All that unreconstituted b.s. scattered around by the "Greatest Generation" (and more recently profitably mythologized by Boomers Tom Brokaw and Tim Russert).

Here's a Billy Joel-esque compendium of the history of the twentieth century to 1960, one that begins in the vast collective memory of that first war that didn't end all wars: another war that didn't end all wars; then a war that didn't end anything; then Joseph McCarthy; Jim Crow; Ethel Rosenberg; Richard Nixon; drive by shootings; college basketball scandals; Rosa Parks jailed; Betty Friedan reviled; Goodman, Schwerner, and Chaney; white bathrooms; Negro bathrooms; white water fountains; Negro water fountains; white schools; ten years after the ovens cooled, Jews traveling to the Pocono who found signs that read, "No Jews or Dogs Allowed"; fallout shelters; keeping up with the Joneses or the Goldbergers, smog-choked cities; dead Great Lakes; Vietnam…and please, please, please don't underestimate the betrayal of the Giants and the Dodgers who abandoned their loyal and profitable fans for the glitzy West Coast. Please.

And, all that while we were pretending we were Ozzie and Harriet or the Reeds or the Andersons.

No wonder the country self-medicated for the rest of the century.

Cut #4

All that to say I honestly don't know for sure why the zeitgeist hit our generation, but there is little doubt that we were different—very different—than the groups that came before us. In my high school, which I suspect was not very different from other high schools around the country, the break occurred between the classes of 1963 and 1964. The class of 1963 belonged—decidedly so—to the 1950s. Button down shirts. Chinos with belts in the back. Mohair. Tassels. Dobie Gillis. My country, right or wrong. Born too late, as the cute Poni-Tails crooned for our yearning ears.

One measly year later, the class of '64 hatched as the personification of the 1960s. We protested the bomb, the early days of Vietnam, even the Pledge of Allegiance. Although some of us were ahead of the curve in high school, we pretty much all went off to college and smoked dope, ate mushrooms, created the notion of the generation gap, and as soon as LSD became as available as candy buttons at the corner candy store, we were the first in line.

Sometimes, I'm tempted to think it was the Kennedy assassination that burst the bubble, that utterly incomprehensible loss of innocence at a time when we were as idealistic as most children ever are, but looking back at Kerouac, Ginsberg, Neal Cassady, the Ban the Bomb protests in England, it had already begun. Kennedy just speeded up the process.

And, what we learned that no one before us had learned (and, sad to say, promptly forgot as soon as we hit the mid-70s or incipient middle age), what goes around comes around…as ye sow, so shall ye reap… everything, turn, turn, turn—déjà vu—Yogi's déjà vu all over again… still crazy after all these years … go ahead, pick your favorite karmic or near karmic phrase about the circle(s) of life and then, go ahead, belt out a riff from Tom Rush's "The Circle Game."

Whatever…as we said back then, karma happens…and as we are all finding out today, karma happens again. And what happened? Despite everyone's wish to stay young forever—i.e., never turn thirty—here we are having skidded through the thirties, forties and fifties, back in the sixties once more.

Bummer.

Well, not necessarily. There are perks to having outlived Janis and Jimi by more years than they lived themselves. Read on.

Cut #5

The actual turning of the annual clock to sixty for me was not a rocky maudlin horror show. No hallucinogenic clips from pasteled senior citizen living (read: dying) communities; no sounds of accordions, or violins, or bagpipes blowing in the wind; no midnight visitations from Neal Cassady, Murray the K, Gurdjief, Ram Dass, Timothy Leary, Nietzsche, Jerry Garcia, Tiny Tim, Jack Kerouac, Carl Jung, Abbie Hoffman, or Edward R. Murrow.

In desperately trying to avoid all the standard trite rationalizations that one might muster up in the months and weeks leading up to the Big Day (e.g, you're only as young as you feel, as long as you've got your health, my kids—or grandkids—keep me young, age is a state of mind, ad nauseum), I did employ a few of the ones more in keeping with the endearing illusions and redemptive delusions associated with being a Baby Boomer:

  • Sixty is the forty of our parents' generation. Given our parents cultural progeria, this actually may be true in spirit—by the time my parents and all the other parents in my neighborhood hit their forties, they all looked like they were waiting for the next car-train to Boca. However, hip as we are, we are sixty, not forty—and if muscle memory serves correctly there's a big gap—a virtual generation gap—in between those ages.

  • Despite what the mirror says, I still feel like nineteen. Sadly true. I have nothing more to add.

  • I still act nineteen. Not always, but more often than is appropriate. Which, somewhat sadly, I continue to say with considerable pride, not remorse.

  • Never trust anyone over seventy (or under forty-five). (Or anyone.)

  • I'm still hipper than my kids. Can you see their eyes rolling into the backs of their heads?

I'll stop there before I really make an abject fool of myself.

However, beyond the delusions, what sixty turned out to be for me was an overwhelming sense of sobriety. (I was going to write utter sobriety, but sober is sober any way you look at it and, let's face it, if you're not high, you're sober.) So, not high. And, not low. Just another day in this imperfect paradise.

Cut #6

Thus, on the anniversary of my actual birthday, Sunday, April 30, 2006, a full sixty years after Lillian A. and Samuel I. Lewis looked at the post-war bundle of promise and misread the goofy smile on my squished face, I didn't take a walk on the cliffs behind our house and contemplate the meaning of "A Whiter Shade of Pale" or "Blonde on Blonde" or "Louie Louie." I didn't attempt Kama Sutra position # 36 in commemoration of the contortions Patti and I once performed in conceiving Clover Anne. (Frankly, I would have had to perform it alone as my wife might actually laugh at me.) I didn't get another tattoo. I didn't make any deals with God, Beelzubub, or even the plastic surgeon to the stars, Steven Hoefflin.

I got up, mainlined some Costa Rican java, mowed the lawn on my nifty John Deere, fixed a light fixture, took a walk on the mountain and, later on, hung out with the kids for a birthday dinner. The next day I went to work. Like so many of our generation that didn't actually plan to ever grow up and consequently don't have a gardener, a handy man, or big fat pension plan, I'm still walking the directionless walk I've been walking for the past forty years.

Cut #7

At twenty, with Hermann Hesse's *Siddhartha* in my back pocket, a Point Beer in one hand, a black cuppajoe in the other, and a joint waiting for me in every apartment in Madison, Wisconsin, I strolled up State Street, figuring I knew everything I would ever need to know about just about everything that mattered. I remember telling my roommate that after all the protests, the happenings, the joints, the music, the loves loved and lost, I felt older than my years. To borrow an eternal line from the master, "I was so much older then, I'm younger than that now." And, despite my wizened world view, I just didn't know that in the next decade I'd be married, have had moved back to the land in upstate New York, and have three kids and one more on the way.

So at thirty, as you might have already guessed, I pretty much figured I had it all figured out. Except the fact that in ten years there would be two career changes, one more high chair around the long kitchen table, and one more kid (the last!) in the oven. So it goes.

At forty, with all that long black curly hair flowing down to my shoulders, I was still imagining myself a latter day Samson…full of the eternal power of me and my locks. I assumed I had the world by hairs, short and long. Except, it turns out, I had overlooked the fact that Delilah—in the form of my unapologetic mother and her cueball-headed brother, Uncle Leonard—had passed along the genetic code for male pattern baldness. And, yes, one more baby. So it goes.

Which brings us to fifty, with all that gray leaping into the tangled mosh pit of whatever hair I had left on my head and those groovy John Lennon prescription glasses amping up my ability to read the writing on the wall if not the small print on the Penguin editions of Shakespeare. I thought I could see the horizon very clearly. In retrospect, it was a clear case of Beatnik myopia

So there I was—here I am—at sixty and I don't need 3-D glasses any more to see what's coming over the hill. I am two steps from the top. Which is three steps away from the big cosmic slide down Space Mountain.

Cut #8

A few weeks after I did the sixty deed pretty much unannounced, my kids all gathered together and invited some of my dearest friends and dearest-related others to join us on a boat sailing in and around the Thimble Islands in Long Island Sound. One miraculous thing—among many miracles of that day—that I had reached sixty years old and never heard of the Thimble Islands in the harbor of Stony Creek, CT, much less seen anything like the hundreds of rocky outcroppings, many with nineteenth century houses perched precariously above the tide line. So, it was like a dream of discovering a new and wonderful room in a house that looks just like your house but when you think back on it the next day didn't resemble it at all.

It was a really nice day, a heartening day. In many ways as nice a day as my memory would have of an earlier birthday, an afternoon at Picnic Point in Lake Mendota, that old cornholer Allen Ginsberg playing his finger cymbals and chanting an exorcism of Lyndon Baines Johnson while the love of my life and I tossed a football back and forth and later...well, you fill in your own blanks.

Cut #9

If there's a deeper message to be found behind this collection of extended riffs on aging hipfully, it's that while it is indeed cosmically good to be cool and mellow; if we learned anything over the past forty years, there are in fact cooler things in life than being cool. As the late and better than great Dylan Thomas wrote prior to drinking himself to death: "Do not go gentle into that good night."

And, while it's somewhat de rigeur to look back on the everything that made us who we were and who we became with an ironic smirk— or an angry sneer—or a holier than thou or some equally goofy notion that they were the best years of our lives—I prefer to look at both sixties (then and now) as the rarest of opportunities to see the universe as it really is—no blinders, no generational illusions, no cocktails, no mushrooms, no Nicodemus, no Nostradamus, no Nietschze.

What it is.

Chapter Two

Fear and Loathing of Boca Raton

Will you still need me, will you still feed me, when I'm sixty-four?
—John, Paul, George, and Ringo

When I turned fifty, my smirking older children presented me with a pair of white shoes, a white leather belt, and a pair of bright green "party pants," just like their grandfather (my father) wore once he and my mother made that elemental trek down the east coast to Boca Raton, Florida. Those same kids also told me, with a little sneer added to the smirk, that they had hoped to find a "Members Only" tan jacket as well, but when they couldn't find a relic in the entire New York metropolitan area, they figured the joke was made already.

It was.

And, the joke was a joke because it was understood that their father would never wear white shoes or green party pants or a Members Only jacket, except at the New Paltz Halloween parade, and I would never ever in a thousand lifetimes end up in Florida, like all my relatives from the previous generation—nor, for that matter, would any of the other aging hipsters they knew in the funky corridor of modern life between New Paltz and Woodstock, NY.

Of course, smart as they were, they didn't know where Patti and I would go once we jumped off the Lou Reed merry-go-round—stick a fork in us, turn us over, we're done. In fact, I don't think they thought that we'd ever really grow up or grow old. But this much is clear, they knew even before they knew that we were not headed toward Boca and all that it represents (fairly or unfairly, I might add):

• Senior Citizens 24-7—Okay, so it's important to state right at the outset that there's nothing wrong with old people. Some of my closest friends blah, blah, blah….I know, older people have wisdom; they have perspective; they are beautiful in a way that can't be bought at a drug store or an operating room. Beautiful with experience. Beautiful with history. Beautiful with story. Beautiful with understanding, their fire and passion and anger burned down to rich burning embers casting a glorious glow on the world around them. (Have I made a good enough case to keep us from being euthanized?) But what is life without babies and bikes and pimples and squeals and sex and fire and passion and anger? Too damnned quiet. And, more importantly, who else but hip elders to model perspective and understanding?

• Gated Communities—This much is clear from the ungated side of life: gated communities don't keep out crime, illness, or death. They keep inmates in. They create fear and paranoia about everything outside the gates. Throw open the gates, comrades!

• Mah Jongg. Canasta. Gin Rummy. Shuffleboard—Need I go on?

• Golf—There's nothing wrong with the game. It's a good game, if sometimes a little exasperating. It takes you outdoors, which is a good thing. It makes you walk (even if you're driving a cart). It's ultimately very social. It requires strength, thought, and concentration—and at the end of a round, it requires a beer and burger. All good things. Everybody I know plays it. I even play it. But every day? Every day? I'm reminded of a woman on Groucho Marx's old television show, "You Bet Your Life," who had eleven children. Marx asked her why she had so many children and she replied sweetly, "Because I love my husband." To which Marx took his cigar from his twisted lips and responded, "I love my cigar, but I take it out of my mouth sometimes."

• Golf Carts—I don't know why, but I just hate golf carts for anything other than golf. Ride a bike or a moped for Christ's sake.

• Aggressive Pastels—Life is not all that cheery all the time. See Chapter Four.

• Early Bird Specials—Frankly, there's a lot to commend this traditional facet of Florida retirement. Early bird specials are cheap, abundant, and, by and large, civilized affairs with no children around. But dinners at 4:30 P.M.? Who eats at 4:30 in the afternoon? And then there's all that yelling—the waitress speaking above the din so that everyone at the table can hear *and* the carping that goes on about the outrageously high cost of low cost meals.

• Ad Nausuem. Add Nausuem.

*

As a card-carrying member of the 69th Ram Dass "Be Here Now" battalion of cultural warriors, I have to step back a pace or two and acknowledge that I never once gave a second thought to any kind of retirement planning. (I had always kind of assumed that one day Patti and I would go out to the barn, turn the key on the old VW bus—the one that had not been started since the mid-nineties—and hit the road toward Nirvana—the place, not the band.)

Apparently, that's not going to happen. That is, I never even considered retirement until very recently, which, as you might well understand, was much too late to start bumping up that TIA-CREFF. However, in skipping over that mile-wide, raging river of missing capital, it was not too late to start considering retirement locales.

*

So let's begin the search for a hipster's retirement paradise with one decidedly non-Chakti Gawain visualization for aging hipsters:

Close your eyes and imagine it's a year or two before retirement, the end of all ends, the beginning of all beginnings, which of course is also the beginning just before the end. You are in the midst of that first exclusively private, rhapsodic moment just after reading some enticing AARP magazine article about the glorious ex-pat lifestyle in San Miguel Allende…or perhaps it's a newspaper piece on active seniors in Sandpoint, Idaho … or you clicked on "12 Great Places to Retire" at Kiplinger.com…or maybe you just got a postcard from Joe and Sandy in their 1,479 foot RV rippin' up the AlCan Highway....

Now lean back and allow yourself to visualize the utter joy of carrying that last box of useless crap out of your office…the simple pleasure of turning the lock on the house that has been sucking up your weekends and vacations and paychecks for most of your adult life…the great relief of tossing the snow shovel, rake, and paid up mortgage into thin air like a latter day Mary Tyler Moore…and, at last, the profoundly gratifying gesture of waving good-bye to the Salvation Army truck with all your useless earthly junk inside (which, I might add, includes the stale air trapped beneath the sofa cushions surrounding all those lost sighs sighed over so many long years, driven by that single-minded intention to act like a responsible adult).

Everything is silent. Everything is still. Everything is necessarily as it should be in the stark presence of Anticipatory Nirvana. This is the Age of Aquarius Redux. You are a flower child again headed to the Golden Gate for the Summer (or more aptly, the Fall) of Love—or perhaps the carefree flower child you weren't allowed to be by your domineering father the first time around. You are fine and funky as funky and fine ever get. You are groovin' on a Sunday afternoon. You got flowers in your hair. You are skippin' the light fandango, trippin' the light fantastic, free from all the stresses, failures, disappointments of real life (and with none of the attendant silliness about nothing left to lose).

Seconds later, though, the bright house lights go up with a *thunk!* and the whole world, it seems, is in on your private reverie. Out of nowhere colleagues whose names you don't even know are sidling up to you at the coffee machine and asking (a sly smirk and an elbow into your side) about your plans for retirement. Indeed, the well-wishers and advice givers are all over the joint, offering cheery "good luck" to you, the startled pre-retiree, who thought you were alone in the midst of some beautiful and transcendent dream.

They are out in the lobby of the apartment building, walking down the street, wandering down the wrong aisles of Home Depot, standing in line at the Grand Union, sitting next to you at the local Property Taxes Are Killing Us (PTAKU) meeting. And it seems that everyone has a comment, a warning, a story, a superstition, a scientific fact, a knowing smile, a pat on the shoulder, a talisman, a friend, a book, an herb, a doctor named Herb. And, amazingly, they're all experts on aging. They know everything there is to know about finances. And nutrition. And senior citizen discounts. And dentures. And early bird specials. And elder hostels.

And geriatric physicians. And bowels. And prostates. And osteoporosis. And warding off Alzheimers. And then that quantum leap into utopia: retirement communities.

So you turn on the tube and find silver-haired after silver-haired folks with twenty-year old skin speaking directly to you about retirement accounts, Eric Clapton or John Mellencamp rocking out—and selling out—in the background. Rugged octogenarians are smiling and waving from kayaks paddling across your computer screens as you surf the net. And with that snappy lead-in to "Gimme Some Lovin'" by the Spencer Davis Group, Dennis Hopper, of all hipsters to sell out body and soul(!), is talking about Ameri-something planning your active retirement because you're not the type to be playing shuffleboard.

In any case, one could drown on the deluge of advice about retirement places alone. It would be overwhelming to any new old hipster trying to enter into the community of others or, for that matter, any couple already staggering under the weight of prescription drugs and adult kids still living upstairs.

Anyone at any age would be confused. And. please know that this particular confusion isn't a function of diminished oxygen to the brain. The amount of free advice out there is so over-the-top that you'd need a brain the size of George Foreman's head just to process all that information.

And, by the way, don't think that just because all the advice is free, it doesn't cost you anything. It costs each of us the confidence that we know what's best for ourselves. Same old story from way back when.

Despite the fact that we live in a culture that is addicted to self-help books and tapes and gurus, there's simply the ordinary confusion of life itself: Even at this advanced age, even for those who have really thought about it, nobody really "gets" it, and paradoxically the more self-help books we read and the more Celestine-esque prophecies we follow the more we mistrust ourselves to find a measure of peace as a person, much less a hip senior citizen. And second, there's the disorientation that all advice invariably creates—simply because experts and would-be experts alike don't seem to agree on anything regarding a normal aging process. Or, what constitutes a healthy and happy existence as a senior. Or, most distressing of all…what it means to live a happy and meaningful life—at any time in life.

So where to go to find your retirement paradise? Read on while considering this one caveat from Larry McMurtry's book, *Paradise*: "…the problem with paradise is monotony. Anyone faced with days, landscapes, seascapes of such unvarying perfection would finally eat the forbidden fruit or commit the sin that would lead to banishment, or at least to neurosis. It would spice things up."

*

Full Disclosure: When I wrote up the proposal for this book, I envisioned this chapter as a great excuse for Patti and me to go traveling around the globe seeking truly funky retirement spots for old hipsters. Just as I have no clear idea of where I'm going to find the money to retire, I had no idea where I might come up with the money for the trip, certainly not from my underwhelming advance, but the dream was very compelling—and in the back of my mind I was already thinking about ways to have local Chambers of Commerce comp our research.

To begin my research I did the usual Google search and found, as I have found with dozens of other issues related to life before and after sixty, that there's a lot more advice out there in the cyber-verse than any self-respecting yogi could contain on the head of a 160-ton pin.

With a few clicks of the mouse I found endless (and I must admit endlessly un-appealing) write-ups on the usual world-renowned retirement communities, from Boca Raton to Phoenix, complete with the usual amenities like world class golf courses, world class medical centers, world-class cultural activities, world-class restaurants, world-class police departments, world-class weather…you get the world-class drift. Of course, they all look alike. The residents all look healthy and happy in their chartreuse shorts, hot pink shirts and full heads of silver WASPy hair, men and women. And, of course, they're all driving those damn cream colored golf carts!

It's enough to make any self-respecting hipster loathe and fear the sixties. (And, thus, the title for this book.)

Yet, please understand that Boca is no more appalling or loathsome than West Palm Beach or Flagstaff or Naples, but as it became the symbol of *the* place where our upwardly aging parents' generation went to live out their lives, it also became the object of my derision. I'll dispense with the elephant-dying-ground jokes, but please know that Boca Raton (literally, the mouth of the rat), represents everything any self-respecting member of the Woodstock Nation rejects: conspicuous consumption, early bird specials, bad driving, white shoes, walled-in communities, "No children allowed," etc.

For any self-respecting hipster to end up in Boca is akin to seeing an old Deadhead driving a Cadillac (read the Introduction if your skipped it). As they say, something is wrong with the picture. I sometimes think moving to one of those retirement communities would be like getting Alzheimers—you never really know where you are because "they all looks alike"—Boca, Ft. Lauderdale, Phoenix, San Diego, yadda yadda...you might as well be in Toledo or Oklahoma City. And, you don't even know who you're with because everyone is dressed the same—and they're all driving, Mercury Marquis.

That said, to be fair, I also found dozens (actually dozens of dozens) of truly surprising and inviting, even exciting, retirement destinations, places where you're likely to see, in addition to old people, a smattering of babies, teenagers, cold weather, people of different color and national original, people with contrasting political beliefs, people of different economic classes, etc. That is, real places with real people.

So, with the map to the next third (?) of my life at my fingertips, I decided to narrow the list by identifying categories that would make retirement/dropping out as laid back as I once imagined it would always be.

- Places with colleges
- Places with good concert venues
- Places with good hospitals
- Places not too far from airports
- Places with good music
- Places with low taxes
- Beautiful places
- Places where famous hipsters hang
- Places where ordinary hipsters are found

Some of the places on what are biblically long lists of Baby Boomer destinations (edited to save you from nodding off while reading) were even surprising. Places like St. George UT, Bellingham, WA, Beaufort, SC, Sarasota, FL, Oxford, MI, Austin, TX, Ithaca, NY, San Luis Obispo, CA, Baltimore, MD (this one really shocked me), Chicago, IL, Denver, CO, Portland, OR, and Asheville, NC. Then there were the offshoots of the ex-pats of San Miguel and Oaxaca: Panama, Costa Rica, "Easy Belize," El Salvador, Honduras, Mexico, Nicaragua, Guatemala, Dominican Republic, "Retire to dirt-cheap Buenos Aires," and Patagonia.

Frankly, my head was spinning right off my shoulders, without benefit of mushrooms or Jimi Hendrix—or booking reservations around the country. The numbers alone are staggering. According to E. Thomas Wetzel, president of Retirement Living Information Center, a website that helps consumers find their ideal retirement spot, "…once boomers start to retire, they will do so at a rate of more than 10,000 a day for the better part of two decades." He goes on to write, "There is no one-size-fits-all plan for this 76-million-strong generation, however. Retirees who relocate generally prefer a safe, uncrowded destination with good medical facilities and a low cost of living. But there is also a nascent trend among retirees to flee the suburbs for downtown to take advantage of all the excitement and conveniences that revitalized cities have to offer."

Yikes!

The sound track for all that advice, which has incidentally also become the sound track for dot com businesses and Mercedes ads, is also vintage 1969. (I'm sorry to report that even the Chambers Brothers, Eric Clapton, and Neil Young are for sale to the highest bidder. And when I saw William Burroughs and Allen Ginsberg shilling for GAP—regardless of their intentions—I knew the world as we once knew it was finished.) In the edgy copy for boomer retirement communities, they always use words like funky, hip, natural, organic, and make reference to things like film festivals and political seminars and pottery classes.

But in the end—as in the end of one's life—there's no difference between retiring in ultra-hip, eco-friendly Door County, Wisconsin, and slappin' on the pastels and car-training it straight to Boca (where the golf and mah jongg set also use the word funky when describing a maverick neighbor who drives a used Beemer and only washes it once a week).

What Kind of Life is the Winnebago Life?

It's tempting, isn't it? Sell everything, buy an ocean liner of a car, slap on the old headband, scoop up all the sounds you'll ever need, grab your old man or your old lady (or both?) and your dog and head out to the great adventure beyond Great Adventure. You're Jack Kerouac, Dean Moriarity, Thelma and Louise (without goofy Harvey Keitel chasing you).

The problem(s): Well, after interviewing several members of the Hell's Winnebagos (names withheld to protect my publisher and me), I found that once you look beyond the great dream of freedom, all that's left are tacky bumper stickers ("I'm spending my grandchildren's inheritance"), the same ol same ol jokes in the form of snow shovels screwed into the bumper with hand written signs (Retired: 4/10/85), a house on wheels that is so damn big it requires towing a car and driving on mega-boring super highways, living quarters smaller than your first pad in Haight-Ashbury and so far less funky that it feels like you stepped into a miniature Motel 6, complete with the glorious smell of Febreze. And, where do you stop for the night? Campgrounds with other monster RVs and their own tacky bumper stickers and retired snow shovels.

Life in a traveling motel room. Stay home.

Sandpoint, Idaho

Along the way I was particularly intrigued by one article from *Business Week Online* titled "Beyond Florida and Arizona: These Aren't Your Father's Retirement Spots …." This piece featured Sandpoint, Idaho.

Mortgage broker Steve Kirby is quoted as saying, "The town itself is a real town." What does that mean? The article goes on to say, "Sandpoint…has been northern Idaho's one relatively liberal, funky outpost, in contrast to the right-wing militias and neo-Nazis who once hunkered down in nearby Hayden Lake."

So aside from the militias and Neo-Nazi thing, Sandpoint hits all the right spots—small, beautiful, water, mountain, outdoor enthusiasts and best of all, just like the good ol' days.

Why does it sound so awful?

*

A story: A few years ago, when we were still young and easy enough under the apple boughs to think that we'd live forever (i.e., we were still in our late forties), Patti and I were busy making plans to get away from it all at a B&B in Vermont. At the time it promised a remarkably rare opportunity for us to be alone in the universe. Having conceived our first child in 1968, minutes after we returned broke from our penniless honeymoon in Paris, we spent the next thirty something years making love and having our spats behind self-made childproof bunkers, which as every parent in existence knows is an oxymoron of moronic proportions. Even the very few times we had gotten away from the large brood, we invariably had to take the infant-at-the-time along with us. (FYI, we have owned a small beachbox of a cottage on Hatteras Island, NC, since 1979, but were never—never—alone there together until the fall of 2005.)

So…Vermont sounded romantic, pastoral, verdant green, full of wild berries, deer and wild turkeys roaming the meadows, so full of maple sugar goodness, and that unique combination of Robert Frost and Bob Newhart pithiness—and so far away from the drama of everyday life here—that I should have been utterly revved up, hot-to-trot, pumped and preened, at the mere promise of my sweet honey and me, all naked and all alone where no one could barge in on us.

Not so. I liked the naked part, of course, but having to cross state lines to do it left me a bit underwhelmed. First, it all seemed pretty expensive. A long drive. A strange lumpy bed. A creaky floor. The sound of showers early in the morning. And worst of all, the obligation to smile and chat with strangers in plaid Woolrich shirts at the charming country breakfast in the homey dining room the next morning.

Ultimately, we realized that we didn't need to leave town to be naked and alone with each other. I'll leave that part to your imagination, but the bottom line was we already lived in a place we loved—and, just as important, felt comfortable in and, more important, loved.

All that to say, I would have done well to remember that sense of absurdity when I first started thinking about potential retirement locales for this book.

*

So back to the question of why Sandpoint, Idaho, sounds so awful: because it's all so disconnected, because life—young life, middle-aged life, old life—is about purposeful connection. Because at the end of the day there is little difference between a rousing game of mah jongg and zig-zagging down the expert slope at Schweitzer Mountain Ski Resort. It's all about filling time. Remember Larry McMurtry.

I recall my 90-year-old father telling me from walled back patio of his two bedroom condo in the Madeira section of Boca Raton, "You're lucky—you have something to do. Playing golf or canasta is not having something to do. Waiting for your kids to show up once a year is not something to do."

Right on. And frankly, I don't think he was talking specifically about filling up his time—no one would ever accuse my father of self-aware-ness. I do think he was telling me how lonely, how disconnected he was from everything that he knew back home. I think he was telling me that as grumpy and grizzly as the old guys seem sitting on a park bench in Rego Park or Evanston or Sacramento—or some faux marble bench in the local Galleria—they are infinitely happier than he was in a supposed paradise where he had no roots, no history, no generational gossip, and no friends except those who were as rootless and unhappy as he.

So, add this to the litany of advice you've already heard: Stay put. Stay home. Uprooted flowers wilt. Work the neighborhood. Move with the flow. Thomas Wolfe might have gotten it right with *You Can't Go Home Again*, but you really don't have to leave. Take day trips. Travel around during the coldest or hottest months.

To quote that flaming sixties liberal, Nancy Reagon, "Just Say No." Don't move. Unless it's absolutely impossible to stay where you are, don't leave the place that you've called home for most of your adult life. I mean, why leave a place where your kids, your friends, your neighbors, your doctors, your pharmacist, are living. Can Taos, New Mexico, a town full of strangers, possibly offer anything other than a good vacation?

As Siddhartha told all of us years—even centuries—ago, you can't escape yourself. And, as Maharishi Mahesh Yogi told us, "Don't just do something, sit there."

Chapter Three

Bankrolling Your Retirement Without a Bankroll

"All you need is love"
—Lennon, McCartney, and my Aunt Miriam

A confession: Much like those visionaries at Decca Records who turned down the Beatles in 1962 ("We don't like their sound. Groups of guitars are on the way out"), at sixty years old I have passed up many more good deals than the twenty-four publishers who initially rejected Theodor Geisel's Dr. Seuss books. I have been at the wrong economic place at the fiscally wrong time in much the same manner as poor old Herbert Hoover during the Depression. I have spent money I don't have, borrowed money I didn't know how I would ever pay back, invested confidently in so many surefire losers based on good vibes that I have had to pawn my good-vibe detector. Such is my life. Such is life, perhaps. And such is life, I suspect, as regards many in our generation whose understanding of economics was based on Abbie's Hoffman's "Steal This Book" brand of capitalism. As such, I am frankly the last person I would turn to for financial advice. But, as "I am you, you are me and we are all together," please read on.

After decades of empirical observation—acquired through many out-of-my-depth discussions with various post-Hippie friends (also out of their depth)—it appears that I am not alone with my financial failures. And, while some economists might at least make the argument that Baby Boomers have been apparently no more—and no less—savvy about financial matters than other generations, there is scant little comfort to be drawn from the notion of universal duncehood, especially when one examines one's losses on paper in the real estate market.

My "missed-the-boat" list probably looks a lot like yours, so let me prostrate myself right off the bat:

• In the mid-late 1970s, Patti and I bailed on a 130-acre property with two houses and a gorgeous barn in New Paltz, New York, which was on the market for the singularly outlandish sum of $107,000. Today, unimproved five-acre lots on that property go for $200,000+. Possible Excuses: a.) Cold feet. b.) Might have to get a regular job to pay the mortgage.

• From 1979 through 2001 (i.e., before the first real real estate feeding frenzy hit the Outer Banks of North Carolina) oceanfront lots on Hatteras Island were going for $30,000. Now—unimproved and threatened by erosion—they're now nearing a cool mill a piece. There's no telling how many we could have bought and sold by now. Excuse: No Excuse (probably too damn lazy to figure out how to do it or perhaps too embarrassed to be capitalists).

• 2001: A six-acre parcel with nice house in Rodanthe, NC, right on Pamlico Sound was going for the "patently ridiculous" (my quotable words) sum of $300,000—which today translates into a conservative $4–6 million. Excuse: No excuse II (feet of clay).

There are more, many more, but let the $10–12 million we've let slip through our hands like so much crude oil suffice. It is what it is.

And that's what it is. Patti and I are sixty years old, up to our snouts in credit card debt and barely (read: not) making ends meet. We're also not in the poorhouse, though, which means that we still have salaries and we have some equity in both houses that we own (actually the credit union still owns one and we own the other) and if I work long enough, we will have enough of a pension and social security to keep us out of the dog food aisle at the local Stop and Shop.

Again…*what it is*—give or take—and *what it is* for many many of us in this anti-materialism generation.

No Whining

Yet, as my eternally disgruntled Aunt Sylvia from Jericho, Long Island (by way of Hollis, Queens), was wont to say, who's complaining?

As much as I sometimes moan about my poor financial acumen, I am not at all unhappy with my lot in life nor do I bemoan where I am and what brought me to this place in my fiscally irresponsible life. As I learned (decade by decade as I have read and re-read Herman Hesse's great treatise on how to acquire the kind of wealth necessary to retire to a houseboat on a river (*Siddhartha*), "… everything is necessary." Every thing *is* necessary because it is only every single thing that has brought you to where you are in the moment that you become aware of it. That would be now.

No Regrets

Indeed, beyond the utterly self-serving and patently self-aggrandizing nature of regret, the only real financial planning tragedies of post-sixty life occur when we experience some non-mushroom inspired flash-back and think that just because we really really really believe it (and have clicked our heels three times) our ship is still coming in. Not so. As Carly Simon once crooned especially for us, "It's too late, baby, it's too late …."

So, with all humility…my first and most important bit of advice: Give it up; if you're not rich, you're never going to be rich. That train has left the station. You're not going to patent the next hoola hoop. You are not going to win the lottery. You're not going to marry a millionaire. Cool and hip and talented as you are, no one is going to just happen upon those cartons of your old tapes, slides, manuscripts, prints, canvases, sketches, treatises, plans for world peace, and/or blueprints for world domination that have been piling up in dusty closets for the past thirty to forty years and pronounce you the winner of the million dollar MacArthur Genius Grant. And, while you're not in danger of waking up one morning and finding that you have turned into a cockroach like Joseph in Kafka's "The Metamorphosis," you are also not going to wake up one day and be transformed into Bob Dylan, Barak Obama, Jack Kerouac, Mimi Farina, Annie Liebowitz, Willem deKooning, Bill Gates, etc.

No. You're going to wake up tomorrow ("God willing," spit, spit, toss the salt, dayeynu) and be one day older. And just as broke as you were the day before.

That's why this chapter is so damn important.

So, my second bit of advice, that is before I get to the people who supposedly know what they're talking about…financial planners—is this four-parter:

1. Stop listening to experts. ("Do I contradict myself? Very well, I contradict myself. I am large. I contain multitudes.") Let me amend that: Stop listening to experts you don't know or don't have your interests at heart. Hip and savvy and "with it" as we supposedly are, the whole country has been sucker punched for decades by bow-tie economists from fancy-sounding think tanks who regularly demonstrate their abject ignorance of the market-place. We've been checked right into the boards by esteemed medical researchers who semi-annually contradict each other's studies on everything from heart disease to cancer to the common cold. We've been conned by politicians from the right and the left about the dangers of slippery slopes. We've been DQ'ed by any number of CEOs at the nation's biggest storefronts (think the esteemed Lee Iacocca, among others) who apparently cannot balance the books without corporate welfare—or outright fraud. And don't get me going on all the foul balls we've chased hit by banks that operate in the red, drug czars who speak as if they're on drugs, hospitals that make sick people sicker, generals who can't punch their way out of paper countries, and hurricane trackers and weather forecasters who don't know which way the wind blows. Bottom Line: Our so-called experts simply do not know what they're talking about.

2. Please stop spending your valuable hard-earned money on the lottery, the single most cynical act of government in our collective lifetimes. It's even more cynical than the annually cynical argument made by millionaires against raising the minimum wage. More cynical than the government's refusal to create national health care. More cynical than all the collective lies about what we were doing in Vietnam…and now in Iraq …and wherever we go next in our quest for planetary control of the fast food market. The lottery is nothing more than state supported greed and more greed—public and private—that preys upon the very people least able to deal with it. That is, the government first makes state supported gambling credible and palatable by promoting the notion that the

lottery helps to fund public education—then entices the middle and lower classes to spend their inadequate paychecks through some slim as 8-pound test line hope of winning a million pounds of greenbacks—and then redirects the profits to pay for everything but public education, including the subsidization of parochial schools. Give it up. If you haven't read the annual expose in the *Poughkeepsie Journal* or the *Des Moines Register* or the *Sacramento Bee*, your chances of winning the lottery are equivalent to your chances of getting hit by lightning. If you like to gamble—or you must gamble—and you don't mind rubbing elbows with people with pinkie rings and anxiety inspired bad breath, go to the track or go to Atlantic City or Vegas or any of the other places now known as "gaming" destinations where they don't lie about where their profit goes and where you actually stand a chance of winning some cash.

Bottom line: As Debra L. Morrison, financial planner (motivational speaker, corporate coach) from northern New Jersey told me, "The research is clear. People feel twice as poorly after a loss than they feel good after an equal dollar gain." Don't poison yourself.

3. Stop beating yourself up over being as irresponsible as your father said you were. (And take some comfort that you're probably a lot happier than he ever was.) You have either been contributing wisely to a reliable retirement fund since you can remember and consequently have enough money (or a lot of money) to coast through the golden years before you drop off the gnarly tree ... or you don't. If you did, bully for you. And if you didn't, you don't—bully for you for making it this far. You're probably going to collect a pension and whatever Social Security you have coming to you, which—assuming the government doesn't rob it from us—is less a safety net than a thin rubber pad to cushion your financial fall upon retirement—and, thus, you must keep on working for the foreseeable future. What it is.

4. Stop buying crap. Don't buy things you don't need. I'm a crap buyer myself, so I know well the lure of warding off the blues or the numbs by buying crap. Gold crap. Silver crap. Antique crap.

Flea market crap. Automobile crap. Sam's Club crap. Hammacher Schlemmer crap. The Sharper Image crap. Aging lotion crap. Penis enhancement crap. Electronic crap. Medical crap. Crappy food. Crappy art. Crappy movies. Plastic dog shit crap.

I also know how difficult it is to stop the crap buying habit in a country where after the horrific attack of September 11, 2001, we were told to go out and buy crap. I guess that was supposed to show Bin Laden and Al Qaeda that we weren't defeated. Nonetheless, as Gertrude Stein might have said in this less elegant age—and Frank Perdue once mimicked—crap is crap is crap. Don't buy it. Crap doesn't turn into gold. Even gold crap doesn't turn into gold. Please consider that idiotic bumper sticker and the yahoos who defile their trucks with it: "He Who Dies With The Most Toys Wins." This is actually one instance where the anti-materialism values of the sixties are truly worth revisiting.

As I mentioned in Chapter 2, there is almost nothing more depressing than watching hapless senior citizens walking around in jived-up, faux hipster towns like Taos, New Mexico, spending their crappy fixed income on crap and more crap from Sharper Image shops. The real bottom line is that we need a lot less crap to live on than we think. Lesser is better—and less really is more.

*

Okay, so enough crap from me. After all the sentimental words about financial independence from every brokerage in the Western world, there is some real world accounting to be done for Boomers on the loose—some of it before you set yourself free, the rest of it after. As someone with a limited future—I know, I know, I know, I should put a more positive spin on that, so let's try …as a person with the best years of his or her life ahead (ahem), you will not only want to be knowl-edgeable and conversant with a wide range of financial issues related to being a solvent older hipster, but in this unforgiving new millennium ethos in which we live today, you will undoubtedly be expected to carry your own weight in the business of your forthcoming old age. That's it. Don't crap around.

After a brief foray into the enduring principals found in Maslow's hierarchy—which I hope will help to explain why the dollars and cents are so important to higher functions such as happiness and self-actualization, I'll move right along to some folks who actually know what they're talking about.

Maslow's Hierarchy Translated into Retirement-Speak

Some of you might remember Maslow's hierarchy of needs from the moments when your REM sleep was interrupted by a required Psych 101 class in college. The theory attempts to explain the dynamics of emotional priorities that motivate people. Without getting into all the psychological mumbo jumbo, the whole thing comes down to this: One cannot pursue higher level needs until more basic functions are satisfied. That is, unless one is free from basic physiological needs (breath, thirst, hunger, bodily comforts, etc.), he or she can't take care of higher level or more complex needs such as safety and security. In the same way, one cannot address even higher level functions of post-sixty hipsterism, such as Belongingness and Love if his or her safety concerns are not completely satisfied.

Maslow's Hierarchy of Needs
Self Actualization
Esteem
Love/Belonging
Safety
Physiological

Ultimately, we all seek happiness and self-fulfillment in life—and some think it is even our due in later life. That is, we worked long and hard, we paid our dues, and now come the rewards. But before we walk up to the bank window and cash in, we each should sit down and consider what Maslow might term the two pillars of stability (Physiological and Safety) before we find anything approaching a sustainable and fulfilling life in the second sixties. For our purposes here, we may say that the Physiological needs are synonymous with Financial Stability and the Safety needs correspond to the health-related issues I address in Chapter Five.

Pillar 1:

As a card-carrying member of the Woodstock Generation, I (and most of my friends) once regarded financial planning as the work of the establishment devil. That was not only an indication of our charming arrogance as a generation, but a sign of our abject ignorance of one of the pillars of a successful family life. (Perhaps another reason so many of my friends are divorced.)

Despite the fact that we love the myth of love and fulfillment transcending money and materialism in this culture ("All you need is love, dumb da da da da...."), life experience demonstrates time and again that money problems have the ability to trump good humor, good sex, good food, and good companionship. Even good health. And, as we understand from Maslow, if you don't have your basic financial house in order, then your real house is in real danger of falling down. Thus, it is in your best interests to understand how to nourish and protect your financial well-being. And that doesn't mean being rich.

In fact, as financial planner (motivational speaker, corporate coach) from northern New Jersey Debra L. Morrison insists, happiness is not a function of having tons of money. (Just look around: There are easily as many or more miserable millionaires than there are truly happy souls just scraping by.) "Anyone," she says, "can be happy if there is a confluence between values and spending in relation to one's assets. Happiness is in coming to terms with your situation." Translation: You can't be happy until you take a long, hard look in the mirror and hip yourself to exactly how much cash you have in your jeans pocket and bank account and pension fund.

Ruth L. Hayden, an internationally known financial consultant from St. Paul, Minnesota, and the author of a wonderfully helpful book on money management, *For Richer, Not Poorer: The Money book For Couples,* told me in an interview that, young or old, the problem is not money itself. "Poor money gets beat up. The truth is that nobody is disagreeing on how much a hundred dollars is worth. What people are disagreeing about is what it should do...and how to talk about it."

Hayden says individuals can head off all sorts of problems simply by learning how to talk about the green. It doesn't matter whether you're married or single, rich or poor, you need to be able to discuss your financial well-being as openly as you talk about your prostate or gall bladder. "Despite the fact that money is the primary motivator for fighting and estrangement in marriage, there is no place in this society where couples learn to talk about money. It is still taboo. In fact, many people would rather talk about their sex life than about money. As a result most people lack the management tools to keep their finances on an even keel."

Morrison agrees completely. She suggests that seniors desperately need to gain control over their emotions before they can gain control over their assets. "Fear is the enemy, not limited funds." And, the first thing to do is to have the courage (her word) to write down what you spend. She advises clients to carry around Post-Its and write down every expense of the day—and to do that for a week or more. "That's how you really find out how you spend your money. It's truly shocking to some people to find out how they fritter away money they need for bills and other necessities." When we take control of those things that are not necessary in our lives (from the $5 latte to the "impulse" purchase in line at Shop Rite to the boredom buy from QVC) we escape the paralyzing fear of not knowing how we are going to pay our own way in life.

Hayden says the way to begin the process is by trying to understand the differences between financial beliefs (emotional) and financial behavior (rational). "Belief statements always involve 'should'—and 98 percent of money statements are belief statements." An example is "No one should spend more than $100 on a meal." That's a belief. In practice, many people can and do spend that kind of money at a restaurant and do not see any moral or ethical sin taking place. A behavior statement is more along the lines of "We don't make enough money to afford to spend $100 on a meal." That's a fact. If it's not in your wallet, you don't have it. Facts have to do with diversification and dollar cost averaging. "Anything more than that slides into emotions and that's where I find that most people stumble."

Morrison adds the sobering fact that since hippies, by and large, have led lives of the "que sera sera, whatever will be will be" variety, it's quite unlikely that any of us will wake up at sixty or sixty-five or seventy and suddenly become financial geniuses. Don't be fooled or fueled by unrealistic expectations. Just as you can no longer dance for the NYC ballet or play third base for the Kansas City Royals, you are not prepared to take a seat on the New York Stock Exchange (or even in your kitchen as a day trader).

Hayden asserts that in that first financial accounting day (of the rest of your life), you—or you and your partner—need to lay your financial cards on the table. Just as important, do not make any judgments about the way you or your partner has managed your money. She says, "If you're willing to have an open dialogue—if you're willing to learn to talk—if you're willing to not always have to be right—then money is just a tool to make your values work to get to your goals."

First, you should make a short list concerning a few very solid facts about your economic position:

1. How much do you make?
2. How much do you take home?
3. What are your regular monthly expenses?
4. How much debt do you carry (credit cards, mortgages, car loans, etc.)?
5. How much equity do you hold—(trusts, real estate, investments, etc.)?
6. What are the realistic prospects of maintaining or increasing your income in the near future?

Once you know where you stand, you can begin the process of turning beliefs into behavior. For example, what are your long- and short-term financial goals? How much debt is acceptable? How much debt can you reasonably handle? Under what circumstances will you use your credit card(s)?

That said, taking your financial temperature should be a regular activity for new or anticipatory retirees. That's why Morrison's idea of carrying around Post-Its is so crucial. It's the only way for people to know exactly what they spend and, in effect, stay hip to their financial well-being.

Chapter Four

Shall I Wear My Bellbottoms Rolled?

"… be sure to wear some flowers in your hair."
—Questionable advice from Scott McKenzie

---

*M*y late Uncle Mac (plaid shirt, checked Bermuda shorts, argyle knee socks, black winged-tip shoes, fat cigar—do I need to mention the silver 1961 Chrysler Imperial?) may not be the fashion poster boy for what Tim Russert and Tom Brokaw have dubbed "The Greatest Generation," but he certainly looked a lot like everyone else's uncle at backyard barbecues during that era.

In contrast to my somewhat nattier Uncle Murray, who liked Hawaiian shirts and whose wife, Betty, laid out his clothes for him before bed each night, I can say with a certain confidence that Mac's memorable outfits were not planned affairs. He could not possibly have thought that the clashing ensemble was attractive or unattractive, and he certainly was not aiming for funky or campy. Nor did his compatriots in the "shoes is shoes, wing-tips go with anything," world.

Indeed, I imagine that in coming-of-age after the profound heartache and disillusionment wrought by the First World War, Maxwell H. Levy and his fellow Americans survived spats, zoot suits, pillbox hats and fringe of all kinds only to find themselves mired in the Great Depression and the kinds of spirit crushing world fascism that rose up in its wake. As such, they are to be excused for having resisted everything and anything to do with artful good taste along the cultural highway. (I have sometimes wondered if they confused fashion with its near homonym neighbor fascism? Who ultimately knows?)

Nevertheless, my uncle's summer weekend wardrobe not only provides us with an indelible, unforgettable vision of the man himself, but as bell bottoms and tie-dyes and headbands are forever connected to the hippie generation, my Uncle Mac's "look" identifies him for eternity as a member of a generation that may well have been color-blind and pattern blind, and they were certainly given to a curious lack of concern for anything that was not functional.

In Mac's world, function trumped everything, aesthetics and nuance be damned; so a shirt was a shirt was a shirt—it covered your hairy chest—and pants were pants—they all go on one leg at a time—and so it follows that socks, white or black, argyle or striped, cover your skinny calves and protect your feet from blisters and your shoes from smelling. End of story. The only things of importance were a good cigar and, of course, to always be sure to wear clean underwear.

From there, we gain some insight into the endemic crew cut, the bland, boxy architecture of the fifties, the cookie-cutter ranch houses, the cream-colored brick high rises, the advent of the TV dinner and the construction of a massively boring interstate highway system. Simply put, after all they had been through, our parents aimed at making their lives easier, more predictable, and more predictably tasteless (i.e., let's satisfy our quenchless hunger—for food, love, beauty, elegance— with some bland three-course something yanked from the frostless freezer and popped into the self-cleaning oven and then drive off to the nameless shopping center in our automatic transmission cars with power steering and power brakes).

Thus also, the neat pile of white starched shirts in my father's dresser drawer, the line of pressed, dark suits in his closet—three brown, three blue, three black—the tie rack full of blue and brown ties, the black belt, the brown belt, the brown shoes, the black shoes, the box with the brown and black Kiwi shoe polish, the grey, black, and brown hats lining the top shelf of the closet in the foyer. (If you want to get a good picture of my father, locate a photograph of the crowd at a baseball game in the forties or fifties, put your finger anywhere in the stands, and there he is.)

Which, following my zigzag line, goes a long long way toward explaining bell-bottoms and the aggressively non-functional, dysfunctional, anti-functional, funk-functional fashion sense that has come to define our generation. (Including, also, a tendency, among some, to skip underwear altogether.)

I don't really need to expound on hippie fashion—as with so much of what's gone on with our cohort, it's been documented and re-documented and mythologized for as long as Mick Jagger has been strutting his bony stuff across stages around the world.

The only thing I need to mention is that the emergence of tie-dyed and floral headbands and bushy hair and the colors of the Jamaican flag were almost Biblical—actually Genesis—like-in scope. From my vantage point as a member of the cross over generation from beatnik to hippie, we moved from basic black (from the beret down to the engineer boots) to a world of color in 1967 or 1968 as we entered the Age of Aquarius, Fifth Dimensionally speaking. That is, from the great Kerouac-Burroughs-Ferlinghetti-ian darkness, the sun reversed course and arose in the west, suddenly bright oranges and reds splashing and spilling across the horizons of our souls—and our clothing.

The interesting turn on all this is that when the Greatest Generation retired and went to Florida, which they did in droves, they too made a profound transformation of color. From those dour browns and blacks and blues, they so easily adopted the *de rigeur* fashion of the aggressively pastel-driven communities of Miami, Fort Lauderdale, Palm Springs, and, of course, Boca Raton: The men wore white shoes, yellow (or chartreuse) Sansabelt slacks, white belt (just in case the Sansabelt wasn't snug enough), chartreuse (or yellow or pink) shirt, and they smoked big fat cigars and, to top it all off, they spread on a nice thick layer of Brylcreem ("a little dab'll do ya"), which I still think is bottled chicken fat or schmaltz. And sometimes, in lieu of hair, they sported an off-color rug covering the bald pate.

Their long suffering wives—and yes, let's be clear, they were long-suffering, and not just in a fashion sense—made a similar transition. Maybe they used the same Florida colors in more convivial and fashionable ways, but know this as well: Too much is too much is too much, and in most cases they could not control their big floral and parrot-motif urges. They looked like blue-headed emus stepping out of their husbands' Coupe de Villes.

*

Okay, so when I stop laughing at all of them, God rest their fashionless souls, I have to take a deep breath and admit that, hip as we are, we might indeed be—actually, scratch that, we are—just as laughable to the twenty- thirty- forty-somethings we created in our sizeable wake. I look at a photo of my big head of hair and jean shirt and burns, a Lucky Strike dangling from my lips—and Patti in her zigzag bell bottoms and fringed leather jacket—and, despite all intentions to stay aground, go "… up up and away in my beautiful balloon…." In turn, my kids—and their kids— look at the photo and actually laugh out loud as if we can't hear them or understand what they mean.

So I apologize in advance for saying this, but take all that Boca pastel, whirl it around in one of those color wheels and voila!...you get tie-dye. Worse still is that we're still wearing the kinds of clothes that once defined us as hippies and beatniks. As a visit to a recent class reunion down on Long Island revealed, maybe the hair and the burns have been lost down the sink drain—or just turned white—and the Lucky Strike lost its appeal decades ago, and we no longer fit into the old bells, but we're still easily identifiable as part of another Members Only Generation. From Judy Goldstein's jean jacket to Richard Gaynor's black t-shirt (more on that later) and black jeans to my ponytail and wrinkled black shirt, we all looked like prod- ucts—or victims—of time lapse photography.

The truth is that generation after generation, we all do that—that is, we wear the clothes that defined us for who we once were forever and ever. Check out all those goofy guys of the seventies and eighties still sporting variations of the mullet and who wear clunky boots and sneak- ers with untied laces. Or…go to any art cinema in any college town or city in the country and observe the sixties' gray and paunchy look.

That's where you'll find me—scraggly, gray hair, ponytail, beard, Levi's, work shirt over a colored t-shirt sitting right behind some guy with scraggly, gray hair, ponytail, beard, Levi's, work shirt over a colored t-shirt—right next to a stunning woman (my lovely wife) with long straight gray hair, little or no makeup, bead necklace, Levi's, Indian pon- cho and sandals who bears a remarkable resemblance to the woman next to the gray-haired guy in front of us.

"Let us go then, you and I" through the "half-deserted streets," the "muttering retreats" of my messy closet: It's like a dusty museum, cum storage locker, of a man's limited clothing sensibilities over the last fifty years. From my pre-hipster, stylistic roots—seventh grade—you'll still find many variations of the button-down Oxford shirt look. And although I left the mohair sweaters behind a long time ago, you'll manage to uncover the khaki pants of my adolescent youth, which I wear when I want to look like a grown-up. (Just so that you know, I know how ridiculous that sounds.) It gets more interesting when you reach down into the dusty corners of the closet and find the work boots, the old leather vest, the faded blue work shirts, etc. of my Madison, Wisconsin years. and the piles of black and blue t-shirts.

My old friend Richard, my best friend since seventh grade and confirmed beatnik of the old school, wears black 24-7. He's been doing that since at least 1970. I'm not exaggerating when I say he must own forty or fifty pairs of black pants and seventy-five or more black t-shirts. He is the poster boy for our time on the fashion runway. His "stuckness" is, in a larger sense, our stuckness: "I am you and you are me and we are all together …."

All of which is to say that I am in no position to make suggestions for making you look natty and dapper and hip into your older age.

And yet, in keeping pace with the charming arrogance of our generation, here I go, at least in reference to male fashions—female fashions to come. Although I can't in all honesty tell you what to wear (just look at me!), I can with utmost confidence recommend what you need to stay away from. Thus, with sincere apologies to Oscar de la Renta, Calvin Klein, Ralph Lauren, Versace, Tommy Hilfiger, Giorgio Armani, Yves Saint Laurent, and *Queer Eye for the Straight Guy*, here goes:

• Clothing designed for anyone too young to drink. Stay away from all labels bearing the logo of FUBU or ecko or enyce or Phatg Farm or any other hiphop clothing company. White or black, you end up looking like an old white geek no matter how cool and handsome you are. Sorry, but you should know that. And, you should know better. Be yourself. Dress yourself. As Gertrude Stein would have said, if only she had gotten the chance,

"You are who you are who are." You grew up in the sixties; there ain't nothing gonna change that—so wear what you think looks good on you—and what your honey thinks makes you look fine and sexy. My Uncle Mac notwithstanding, the only people who look patently stupid are the sixty- and seventy-year-olds wearing today's fashions.

• No tie-dye, no headbands—except while jogging, and even then, only at twilight—no bells, no shirts with Peter Max scenes. No granny glasses. Ankle bells are so out. No fringed leather vests. You want to look like someone of substance, someone with some hip about him, not a relic or a Saturday Night Live bit or Sonny Bono. That said, a modest, understated non-Al Sharpton-sized peace symbol is, if not always appropriate, never inappropriate.

• Don't buy old people's fashions because that's what the stores offer senior citizens. North and South, there is simply far too much polyester in the men's sections of department stores. In the North, Midwest, and West, there is too much reliance on neutral colors. Older people look washed out in tans. In the South and Southwest, where they love pastels, please know this: big flowers and/or big birds make thin hipsters look punier than they are and large hipsters look larger than Kate Smith. You don't have to look dowdy.

• I know it makes life much easier, but I would suggest avoiding all Velcro, especially when it comes to footwear. Try shoes you can slip into, like Merrills

• Workshirts. Forgive me, but those light blue, faded workshirts are a classic of laid-back hipness. With or without a tie. (No string ties allowed.) Never out of style, in part because after 1969 they were never in style. Granted, my friend Bruce Schenker's grown children forbid him from wearing his favorite workshirt(s), but what do they know?

• Levi's. Yes. Yes. Yes. Wear the old Levi's, but please don't feel free to pull them all the way up to your nipples—or let them fall below your fallen butt.

• No lamb chop sideburns. No Rollie Fingers mustaches.
• No boatneck shirts.
• No leather pants.

- And, of course, NO COMBOVERS! #$%^&*&>?!

Okay that's it. A quick summary: Don't dress like an old person. Don't dress like a young person. Don't dress like you're headed off to Woodstock, 1969.

An Additional Note about Combovers

You're not fooling anyone. Remember this:

Five-year-old Devin climbs up in the big barber's chair in Saugerties, NY, sits up straight like the big boy that his mommy wants him to be, and then waits patiently as the barber swings the sheet around his shoulders like a matador in training. The big boy smiles sweetly at his mother while the barber snaps the sheet around his thin neck and pumps the chair up to the right height to give big boys' haircuts.

When the barber says in his most kindly barber voice, "What kind of haircut would you like this time, Devin?" Devin doesn't shrug like he usually does. He knows exactly what he wants. He's already thought about it at home and on the ride over to the barber shop in the backseat of the Volvo. "I'll have a circle," he says.

"Circle?" asks the confused barber.

"Circle?" asks his confounded mother Melissa, suddenly fearful her beautiful blond boy has been tricked once again by his tricky older brother Clay.

"Circle," replies the boy, confident that he has come up with the perfect haircut.

The barber presses his lips together and looks toward Melissa for some guidance. "Devin," she begins haltingly, "you know, we're not sure what a circle haircut looks like. Try to describe it, okay?"

Devin is now the one wearing the look of consternation. (I mean, how could two adults not know what a circle is?) "A circle," he repeats a little patronizingly.

"A circle?"

"Yep, a circle." He waits a few seconds to see if they finally get it, but they don't: "... like Chief."

Oh? Ohhhhhhhhhhhh! Melissa gets it, but the barber is still confused. "Who's Chief?" he says.

"Devin's grandfather," Melissa murmurs, not knowing whether to laugh or scoop up her kid and run out of the shop. "The kids call him Chief…and, well, he's pretty well bald on top…like a circle, I guess."

"Ahhhhhh…." the barber nods and smirks—at what parts of the information he has learned, we're still not sure. Then he proceeds to give Devin the buzz cut he was going to get anyway. Like all the little big boys in Saugerties.

But that's not the end of the story. Back at home in the woods, where the story was told a few days later with a dollop too much glee by my oldest son Cael and his wife—and received by the big family sitting around the long dining room table with more than a gravy boat of hilarity at the bald guy's expense—I humbly learned a late-in-life lesson—and not just the making lemonade out of the lemons thing—or the beauty is in the eye of the beholder thing—or the love is blind thing—or even the "Hey, ya never know" thing. It's all that, but it's also this:

I am a man who happily and hairfully came of age in the long-hair sixties, a man who felt a biblical kinship with Samson and, not withstanding his own better and hipper tastes, always sang joyfully along with the Cowsills and their love of "…long, straight, curly, fuzzy, snaggy, shaggy, ratty, matty, oily, greasy, fleecy, shining, gleaming, steaming, flaxen, waxen, knotted, polka-dotted; twisted, beaded, braided, powdered, flowered, and confettied, bangled, tangled, spangled and spaghettied!"—hair, that is.

I also believed in my John Lennon heart and soul that "Love is All You Need"; and nearly forty years later as a Woodstock Generation grandparent my spirit still glows when I hear Steve Miller sing about the "pompitous of love."

The problem was that I somehow connected the two, hair and love. In all those years since that hairy Summer of Love, as I have observed morning by rueful morning, cold month through hot month, good year by bad year, awful president by worse than awful president, my long, brown, curly hair turning gray and falling out, I became increasingly distraught at my own follickly-impaired slide into the land of the bald and homely—and worst of all unloved.

And then this innocent, fair-haired four year old, who loves me for no other reason than I am his beloved grandfather, comes along to let me know (through his wise-cracking parents and aunts and uncles and a barber I have never met) that someone out there not only thinks I'm still lovably hip, but that the universe is perfectly round—a beautiful circle. Bald baby, bald!

*

And that said, please know that I do have some boundaries—and some humility: So it was to my friend Richard's daughter, the uber-beautiful Violet Moon Gaynor, fashion editor of Luckymag.com, and gorgeous and urbane Isabel Burton, deputy editor of *Cosmopolitan*, whom I turned to for post-sixty fashion advice for women.

Violet Moon Gaynor's Post-60 Do's and Don'ts

The age-old question of "What to wear?" takes on new meaning with each approaching milestone year. At twenty-one, the question may involve how to trade in relaxed college attire for a more formal work-appropriate wardrobe. At sixty, this question poses no less of a quandary. When the rules have suddenly changed and the dress code seems to be written in a foreign language, take a step back and reassess. Follow along for the simplest instructions for dressing the part (and don't forget—sixty is the new thirty! [Or something like that]):

Fashion

• **Do** Buy black turtlenecks in bulk (they elegantly cover the ever-changing neck area and go with just about everything).

• **Do** Invest in designer classics such as a men's wear inspired button-down shirts and a perfectly cut pair of trousers. Carolina Herrera and Oscar de la Renta know a thing or two about tailoring, let them be your guides.

• **Don't** Over-spend on closet staples, there's no reason to—Diane vonFurstenberg's wrap-dresses (in-style since the 1970s) cost around $300 and are universally flattering. Wear these with flat sandals in the spring and summer, and with opaque stockings and your favorite boots all fall and winter long.

• **Do** Find a good tailor. They can take shoulder pads out of jackets and pleats out of pants, instantly updating old favorites.

• **Do** Clean out your closet. The editing process is key to an updated wardrobe. If you have to ask yourself whether or not to hold onto that old pair of cropped leggings, the answer is probably "no."

• **Don't** Give in to fads—fashion victim is just as bad at 60 as it was at 20.

• **Don't** Bring back your "skinny jeans" just because you've shed a few pounds and they fit. Newer styles with features like a slightly lower waist, a slimmer leg and the strategic placement of side seams create an instantly leaner silhouette—and you won't have to do half an hour of stretching to make them fit!

• **Do** Know what looks best on your figure and stick with it. Straight-leg trousers are always a classic, even if an ultra skinny-leg is all omnipresent in the runways and in the magazines.

Beauty

• **Do** Update your look—invest in a great salon cut and color. And always bring along a picture of your ideal style. Your idea of a shoulder-sweeping bob may be different from your stylist's.

• **Don't** Stick to the same regime you've followed since college—skin's elasticity and coloring changes with age, adjust your products accordingly.

• **Don't** Wear blue eye shadow—it's never O.K.

• **Don't** Skimp on what you put on your face—drugstore brands don't always cut it. Figure out what works best for you.

• **Do** Clean out your makeup bag—ten-year-old purple eyeliners and dried-up red lipsticks belong in the trash. Make room for newer, lighter formulas like soft shadows and sheer glosses that add brightness to the face.

• **Don't** Pile on the foundation. Thicker formulas have a way of magnifying fine lines. Instead, choose light, water-based products that glide over skin and hide imperfections without appearing mask-like.

• **Do** Slather on a moisturizer with SPF 365 days a year. Though 80 percent of sun exposure is acquired by the age of 18; it's never too late to ward off additional wrinkles, pigmentation, and even skin cancer.

• **Do** Embrace your looks by playing up your best assets.

Love your shiny, wavy locks? Then wear your hair long and down! Want to draw attention to your elegant collarbone? Then don't be afraid to wear a plunging neckline and apply a sweep of shimmering powder that puts it on full display! And remember, having fun with your looks is always a resounding yes!

Hold On There, Cowgirl...Advice from Isabel Burton

• Ladies, give long hair a chance. Noted, short hair is easy, sensible, it dries quickly after water aerobics, but unless you're pulling off a stylish pixie, the helmet-head look won't do you any favors. This is politician hair; it's got mass appeal because it's boooring. Consider growing it out, doing an elegant bun, even a low, classic pony. Nothing fussy, just a bit more glam, than say, Sandra Day O'Connor.

• Lay off the elastic. It's a bit evil that clothing made for "mature" women includes so much elastic (waistbands, ankle gatherings…), the very thing that turns your figure into a Schmoo. Stay strong because this is tempting stuff: No complicated buckles! Oh, yes, so comfy! But back away, seriously. It's worth the effort of buttoning and zipping to look human again.

• Which leads to another important must: structure. Look for clothing that has a little stiffness, a little architecture, especially if you're sporting any sort of stomach paunch. And really, aren't we all? Soft, floppy material will skim the area and create a sandbar effect. Not flattering. But material slightly less giving will mask lumps, bumps, and anything else weird that's going on under there.

• Lipstick is not a universal fix-it. Often, women will swipe on that loud Estee Lauder pink and think they're good to go. Hold on there, Cowgirl. Bright mouth on a bare face acts like a beacon, drawing the eye to every line and crease surrounding your possibly thinning lips. It makes you look witchy. The name of the game here is: diversify. Keep the eye moving by spreading out your makeup. Some light foundation, blush (easy does it—*you're* closing in on seventy, it's not *the* seventies), eye shadow, and then, a nice natural lip shade. You'll look pretty, not pouty.

And groovy, I might add.

Chapter Five

Being and Healthiness: A New Wrinkle on Kierkegaard

"Doctor, doctor, what's ailing me?"
—The (no longer) Young Rascals

---

*F*irst, an eternal truism from my dear departed Aunt Miriam (wife of the fashion maven Uncle Mac from Chapter Four): "As long as you've got your health…." (Note: I didn't insert the ellipses—she just never finished the sentence.)

Everyone always knew what she meant, though, which is that you simply can't enjoy your life if you're not feeling well. And just about everything follows from that simple premise, including the precious fact that you won't enjoy your grandchildren—and vice-versa—if you're not only healthy but feeling alive and well.

So, I'd like to begin this chapter with a cautionary tale about my rather cavalier attitude toward the concept of health maintenance after age fifty. It begins with the voice of my family physician at the time:

"Steve, your cholesterol level is still too high," the good Dr. Gerber muttered from behind the lab report in front of his face. "Now I have to *insist* that you go on medication."

My fifty-six year-old inner teenager slumped in abject failure. Despite more than ten years of unsatisfactory blood panels I had somehow managed to successfully dodge the doctor's prescription pad and the heart-rending notion of taking a pill every day for the rest of my life. At each annual physical, generally held every two to four years, I had cholesterol readings in the 250 plus neighborhood (a place one doesn't live too long). Nevertheless, at each appointment I had solemnly promised to eat better and exercise more. I knew I could reduce the cholesterol levels through diet and exercise. I reminded the good doctor that I actually did it once back in '95. Further, as a father and health educator, I explained to the increasingly skeptical physician, I had an obligation to my children and my students to be a role model of healthy living. Not a passive pill popper.

Unfortunately, as my thickening file full of red-flagged lipids profiles demonstrated beyond any shadow of an artery-clogging doubt, I hadn't been good to my word.

The doctor was already writing on his prescription pad when I realized that I had used up all my excuses, including the classic, the dog ate my tofu. "And please fill it," he intoned, glancing ominously over his glasses as he extended the slip of paper in my direction. Before he actually let go of the paper to my grasping thumb and forefinger, he proffered a cautionary tale about a former patient "generally in good health, like you," eyebrows raised, "and with similarly high cholesterol readings..." who had been putting off the medication question for years.

Of course, you know where this is going ... my LDL brother apparently folded and slipped the small note into his breast pocket, but never actually made it to the pharmacy. Then some unspecified time later the unlucky or unwise or cavalier sap dropped dead, face down in his lobster bisque.

I'm sure the doctor assumed I was standing there shuddering with intimations of my own mortality. Or at the very least I might have been grateful that the doctor had grabbed the invasive menace—and my attention—before I clogged all my arteries and fell to the pavement like a lump of chopped liver.

Not I. I may be the walking embodiment of everything that is wrong with this culture. I was menu planning. Despite the fact that I'm New Age enough to recognize a good clump of tofu when I see it—and I even sometimes teach courses in health philosophy—I am also a red-blooded American and with a pound or two of sugar I can turn any number of lemons into lemonade.

So, there I was pushing through the heavy medical office door, barely able to contain my glee, much less my urge to grab a light pole and dance. After wrestling for years to find the mystical 200 cholesterol level through various half-hearted commitments to jogging, biking, carrot sticks, sprouts, rice cakes, herbal potions, and more turkey sandwiches (with mustard) than the USDA recommends for small countries, I was hungry for the magic pill. Freed from the psycho-sclerotic notion that natural remedies are best and that personal responsibility is the hallmark of good health, my unrequited love of mayonnaise, bacon, pastrami, egg salad, prime rib, deep fried anything, and mucus-producing dairy products of all kinds had me drooling.

Loaded for bear fat—or fat of any kind—I headed straight to the local drug store to double-check with my ace-pharmacist Jack about potential side-effects that the doctor might not have mentioned (or known about). Once satisfied that I was not trading food for other worldly plea-sures, I popped a tablet into my mouth and headed straight to McDonald's dreaming of a scrumptious Big Mac, super-sized fries and, a large Coke. And a big Ahhhh. And a cosmic Ohhhh.

As you might imagine, the drive to the Golden Arches was fueled by powerful primitive urges—and their drooling counterparts. And much like the predictable period of sexual promiscuity normally associated with recently divorced men and women, I left McDonalds and went on to live the dream of the insatiable doughnut glutton, the chip 'n' dip hedonist, the all-you-can-eat fast food slut. With this daily chemical additive sup-posedly cleaning out my arteries like a can of Liquid Plumber, I quickly became the self-satisfied, waddling embodiment of everything the Fed-eral Reserve asks of all loyal Americans: Consume! Consume! Consume!

I'd be lying if I said it wasn't a great few weeks of complete nutri-tional debauchery. You name it and I ate it—and loved every bone-suck-ing, sugar-swilling minute of it. Yet, I'd be also lying if I didn't tell you that within a couple of days of my non-stop grease diet I grew as gassy as the family dog—and a few days later I started to feel too loggy to climb up on my bike for a ride into town—and then, insult added to dietary injury, three weeks after I began my binge I began to feel too achy and tired to get off the couch when I heard my oldest grandsons, Clay and Devin, race through the front door looking for their Chief to wrestle them down to the floor. I held out my arms and invited them onto the couch with me. They just turned and looked for their grandmother who had some cookies for them.

Thus, it came to pass a mere three weeks after I inhaled that first Big Mac with such unrepentant gusto, I had my first super-sized revelation about the links between post-fifty health maintenance and healthy relationships with one's grandchildren.

According to Annemarie Colbin, author of *Food and Healing* and *Food and Our Bones: The Natural Way to Prevent Osteoporosis*, the real reason I felt so horrible was nothing less than a direct result of the excessive sugars, salts, and carbohydrates in each bite of my super-sized Big Mac Meal ... and let's not fail to mention the scrumptious chalupas from Taco Bell ... and the extra crispy chicken from the Colonel ... and the three Sabrett's hot dogs (mustard and kraut, please) from the street vendor in Manhattan ... or the resulting lack of exercise ... and the subsequent lack of sleep ... and the extremely windy and sulfuric consequences of what our parents' generation would have politely called irregularity.

As a younger man, I guess I could get away with poor dietary health habits and still lead an active life. But there right in front of me was a stark fact of life: At fifty-six, much less sixty-six or seventy-six, I realized that I can't be stuffing my pie hole with all sorts of empty, gooey, pointless calories and expect to be an alert, involved spouse, parent, or grandparent. Not any more. Not any more.

So, give me that big V-8 slap on the forehead ... there really is a lesson in all this: After age fifty, it's no longer just about being healthy for the sake of being healthy (which is not a bad idea, but it seldom works). And after age sixty, it's only about being healthy enough to enjoy your life, your pleasures, your grandchildren—to be a real presence in their lives, not just be a snoring overstuffed pillow on the couch—or God forbid, a sigh-inducing chore or burden. Clearly, health is its own reward, but being healthy for a senior citizen makes the critical difference between enjoying life and finding it tiring. And, for those with grandchildren, it's worse than that: It's them finding us tiring.

So, if we want to enjoy the life we've earned, we really do have to take care of ourselves.

It all starts with having the energy to do what we need to do to keep ourselves alert, involved, and alive. Beyond actual illness and injury and the normal effects of aging, one of the major obstacles to seniors taking control of their lives is simple fatigue. In fact, it may be the most common senior citizen complaint: I'm tired. I don't have the get-up-and-go, the pep I used to have. It takes too much energy just to get out of the house these days. Sound familiar?

Although it is generally assumed that fatigue is a most unfortunate but unavoidable function of aging, that notion is pretty much an old (or young) wives' tale. As it turns out, being older does not require being more tired.

Combating Fatigue

Michael Freedman, M.D., a gerontologist at NYU Medical School, writes that it's a myth that fatigue is necessarily a function of aging. "With normal aging, not a heck of a lot changes in terms of one's energy levels.... It may surprise you to know that generally healthy people in their 80s and 90s should have pretty much the same energy levels they always had."

Well, if that's true—and practically all my research suggests it is—the first thing any of us needs to do is to get up off the couch and examine why we're so damn tired. I know, I know, I know ... that kind of self-examination takes energy (and we all thought we were finished with the tedious process of self-examination back in the eighties), but it's pretty clear that the only way any of us will actually find the missing energy is to look it right in the eye.

Building upon a recent AARP report on loss of energy in senior citizens, I found that there are ten typical culprits that rob us of our zest. [Grandparental Advisory: The first three on the list you can experiment with on your own. The following seven should be diagnosed in conjunction with your doctors]:

• **Minor Dehydration**—This axiom is as old as your grandmother's grandmother—each of us needs to drink eight cups of water a day. If we don't, our energy levels are sapped (less sweating, heart pumps less blood to skin, core body temperature rises ... all leading to energy drain). There are only two rules to follow in order to get yourself properly hydrated: 1.) Don't count alcoholic or caffeinated beverages in your eight count—both can dry you out. 2.) Consider your bladder habits and do most of your eight glasses before dinner time. (It's hard to get a good night's sleep when you're getting up to go to the bathroom every other hour.

• **Late Night Indulgences**—Eating too much too close to bedtime can and will interfere with restful sleep. You know this, you knew this decades ago, your mother might have even warned you about nightmares and late night snacks. But you probably didn't believe her then—and you probably still don't believe it today. Believe her now. If you must eat late, good before-bed foods include milk, yogurt, cheese, turkey, and fish. They all contain the amino acid tryptophan, which converts to serotonin in the brain, making you feel drowsy. Don't, however, take liquor before going to sleep as a way to combat fatigue. Liquor will make you feel tired, but it will also interfere with your REM sleep, which is the refreshing part of sleep. As your mother said a long, long, long time ago, you need your sleep. And as your father said (pointing his finger), get to sleep now!

• **Simple boredom**—This one is another no-brainer. "The more you just lie around, the less likely you are to get up," says health educator and retired athletic director at Marist College, Howard Goldman, Ph.D. Young or old, when you have nothing to do, you end up napping. And the more you nap, the more you nap. And the more you nap. So, just don't sit there, do something. Fix something in the house—something is always broken. Go to a museum, a ball park, a mall. Join a birder's group, a hiking group, an AARP group, a political party. Anything. Get a puppy. Volunteer at Meals on Wheels or the hospital or the local crisis center. Get a job at the bookstore. Get off your ass. Dr. Goldman, who's been retired for eight years, plays golf regularly, teaches an occasional course at the local college, travels, and volunteers on several local boards. "Whatever you do," he says, "get involved. Get the juices flowing. Wake up and get the blood flowing."

Still Tired? Now Go See Your Physician to Check on One of These:

• **Low Blood Pressure**—This one is relatively simple. According to a report in the *British Medical Journal*, fatigue is common in people with low blood pressure. Symptoms include frequent tiredness and light-headedness. The report quotes Johns Hopkins School of Medicine cardiologist Hugh Caulkins who says the simplest solution to hypotension induced fatigue could be adding plain salt to your diet. Check with your physician before doing anything.

• **Sleep Apnea**—It stands to reason that if you don't get enough sleep—or don't get enough good sleep—you're just simply going to be tired. Although there are as many reasons for poor quality sleep as there are nights in the year, one cause that is frequently overlooked is sleep apnea, which is often characterized by heavy snoring. A person with sleep apnea stops breathing many times a night which partially arouses him from sleep. He never really gets a good night's sleep. However, often the poor fellow doesn't recognize it's happening. Robert Chervin, M.D., University of Michigan neurologist, reported in the medical journal *Chest* that sleep apnea occurs in one in four men and one in ten women. And the editors of the University of California, Berkeley, *Wellness Letter* say that a 100 million Americans snore. So if you're always tired and your husband or wife—or significant other—has been complaining about the nasal symphony you've been performing every night for the past umpteen years, you might very well be one of them. Get it checked out. It's one of those things that can't hurt. (It also might account for your spouse's daytime weariness!)

• **Low Testosterone**—Here is one startling fact: One in three men over sixty-five has low testosterone levels—low enough, that is, to account for unusual fatigue. A simple blood test will determine your testosterone level. The two-fold solution is often quite simple (taking a pill) and pleasurable (engaging in more sex). Thus, the line eighteen-year-old boys have always given girls about "needing" sex, actually might have some validity forty, fifty, sixty years later.

• **Thyroid Problems**—In my research I have found that 10 to 20 percent of older adults produce too little thyroid hormone. The result? You feel beat all the time. You might even notice a lack of "luster" in your skin and hair—or a new intolerance to cold. Go see the doc.

• **Anemia**—Anemia is a blood condition that is characterized by insufficient levels of hemoglobin. Forget the tenth-grade biology lesson: All you really need to know is that one of the prime symptoms of anemia is fatigue. In younger people there are several causes of anemia, but in older adults it's usually associated with minor internal bleeding caused by the liberal use of aspirin or anti-inflammatory drugs, or ulcers or hemorrhoids (sound familiar?). Whatever the cause, though, anemia is often easily diagnosed with a blood test—and generally easily fixable. As above, check with your doctor.

• **Eye Strain**—My hipster optometrist, Dr. Bruce Schenker, O.D., reports that eye strain is a common cause of weariness—and not just among older people. "Whether you strain your eyes as a result of improper prescriptions or from sitting for hours in front of a computer screen, the solution is relatively simple: Make sure you have an annual eye checkup—and, like they say with regard to eating and physical activity … everything in moderation—including reading, watching television, and surfing the web." As above, make an appointment to get your eyes checked. It could make all the difference in the way that you view your world.

• **Your Prescription *and* Non-Prescription Medicine**— Lurking right in your medicine cabinet might be the real source of your fatigue. Common energy robbers include medications for hypertension (high blood pressure), anxiety, and infection. Again, check with your doctor—or better still, check with your doctor and your pharmacist. (Frankly, I never take anything that's been prescribed for me without talking to Jack or Bill Sheeley at Dedrick's Pharmacy—see Chapter 10).

Then There Are All Those Aches and Pains

As Homer wrote a billion years ago (or so) in *The Odyssey,* "For fate has wove the thread of life with pain." And as Bruce Schenker told me at my last visit when I looked shocked that I needed trifocals, "The warranty is off, Steve. From now on things are going to periodically break or break down. Get used to it."

By fifty (and definitely by sixty), we all understand that some measure of chronic pain is an everyday part of growing older. Whether it's a touch of arthritis, an old injury, muscle stiffness, hemorrhoids, or some other non-acute condition, we simply don't bounce back as easily as we once did. That means we often don't bounce at all when the grandkids want to bounce. And that's a shame.

John Giglio, executive director of the American Pain Foundation, asserts that fifty million Americans suffer from chronic pain, and another twenty-five million suffer acute pain: "And there is no question that older folks suffer a disproportionate amount of pain."

Adding to the burden, many of us suffer under the old Protestant Work Ethic notion that we're supposed to keep a "stiff upper lip" and just accept our fate without complaining. Not true. Take a load off, Fanny. Although there is no foolproof way to avoid some pain, there are multidisciplinary programs that help many people rise above their pain enough to lead active, happy lives. There include medication, exercise, biofeedback, and psychotherapy.

In any case, if you hurt, have a frank talk with your physician. Then go get a second or third opinion. Find out if there's anything you can do to relieve your pain. If there's no solution, go see a counselor to help you live well despite it. And here's where we enter the existential world grandparental life.

Just Do It: Some Thoughts on Existential Health

Robert Steinfeld, M.D., a former vascular surgeon presently specializing in complementary therapy, asserts that there are no magic bullets for feeling strong and healthy—especially for the geriatric crowd, however hip we may be. It's not enough to just take care of the ten culprits for fatigue, pop an analgesic, and then lie back and turn on the television, figuring you've done all you could. If you want to play (cook with, travel with, etc.) with your grandkids, you have to lead a healthy lifestyle.

As we age, it becomes less and less acceptable to just sit back and accept what life throws at us. This is particularly important because we live in a society that believes in the "magic bullet" version of medicine. Got a pain? Take a pill. Get an operation. Unfortunately, that relatively passive approach not only doesn't work very well, but actually weakens our ability to heal ourselves.

"It's all about taking an active role in your own well-being," Dr. Steinfeld counsels. "Being healthy essentially amounts to a holistic three-pronged approach to living well," he says, referring to the mind, body, and spirit. "And it's not just enough to take adequate care of your body;

you have nourish your mind and your spirit as well." Study after study demonstrates that the body-mind connection is not science fiction or New Age wishful thinking. If your body is not functioning properly, it will have an enormous effect on your state of mind—and your spirit. And it follows that if you are emotionally overwrought—or spiritually ill at ease—your body is bound to suffer as well. That's not rocket science. It's simple age-old truth. Anyone who has managed to stay alive for more than fifty years should have learned that along the way.

Unfortunately, there are no magic bullets or guaranteed programs to protect us from all injury and disease. (Sorry about that!) But as my experience taking cholesterol meds demonstrated, taking charge of my life was the key to living well in the moment. The pill will predictably help keep me alive in the long run, but I still had to change my diet to be healthy.

Although it often seems that the medical community is constantly feeding us contradictory messages about how best to take care of ourselves (caffeine-no caffeine, high carbs-no carbs, an hour of exercise per day-an hour per week, etc.), there are some relatively simple basic principles of healthy living upon which almost all practitioners seem to agree. That is, simple guidelines that that will allow each of us to feel as good as we possibly can given our individual circumstances—as good as we should feel—and as good as our grandchildren want us to feel. Eat, drink, and be happy.

How About Sane and Tasty Nutrition?

Few health problems and issues are addressed any easier than identifying a healthy diet—and few health regimens are more difficult to follow than strict diets. Back in the old back-to-the-land era in the early-to mid-seventies, we might have overstated the "you are what you eat" message. It's kind of a catchy concept, but it doesn't hold up to scientific or cultural scrutiny. However, with some hindsight and slightly more than a dash of wisdom gleaned over thirty years teaching health principles, I have come to a new understanding of that old hippie concept: How we eat says a great deal about how we live our lives and maybe even who we are. Gluttons are gluttons are gluttons are gluttonous no matter what foods they're consuming; and those who choose to eat severely restricted diets (without sound medical reason) lead severely restricted lives. Thus, we all have to find a nutritional middle ground for real people eating real food.

Being healthy does not doom you to a lifetime of tofu and cardboard rice cakes ... and balance does not mean coordinating your daily dose of prunes and Total cereal. Eating well is one of life's distinct sensual pleasures—one that can be enjoyed across the entire lifespan—and it should never become a dull and tasteless task. As a guiding principle for your nutritional well-being, you certainly don't have to give up everything you love to eat in order to eat well. Ice cream is not only tasty, it's good for the soul.

Mens Sana in Corpore Sano, Yo!

The age-old prescription from the Greeks still stands as the essential foundation for healthy living: Everything in moderation. The failure of almost all diets is that they demand too much; they're too hard (and often too tasteless) to sustain. For example, if you notice that red meat makes you weary or loggy an hour or two after eating, but you still enjoy and want to eat read meat, bully for you. Just don't eat red meat every day—and try to eat a little less of it when you do indulge—and, just as important, try to eat meat that isn't so full of hormones and antibiotics that you're in danger of growing hair on the soles of your feet.

Stop any mainstream dietary consultant on the street and you'll get the same message: more frequent and smaller meals. This is not radical nutrition; it's been a known entity for decades. Nevertheless, whether it is old or new news to you, it should mark, for all intents and purposes, the end of heavy meals at night—even if they're late early-bird specials. Fact: there is not an early enough early bird to catch this particular worm.

Get Off Your Ass

According to recent clinical trials at Harvard Medical School, moderate exercise (jogging one hour per week, rowing one hour per week, walking a half hour per day, etc.) not only reduces one's risk of heart disease, but enhances the quality of your everyday life. So, you don't have to run marathons or climb mountains or surf the Great Barrier Reef. Just get off your duff on a regular basis and you'll not only feel better, but you'll be able to get off your duff easier and perhaps without that give-away groan that we hear from most old duffers. Everything in moderation.

The Mind is a Terrible Thing to Let Atrophy

Let's be clear, it's not just muscles that atrophy from disuse. The brain is an organ that thrives when it is challenged—and, frankly, grows limp when it snoozes. Carole Ford, professor emeritus at SUNY-Empire State College and expert in adult education, tells us that there are endless ways that older adults can use to keep their minds healthy and alive. She reels off a list possibilities, including adult education classes, writing, traveling, memory programs, crossword puzzles, reading, discussion groups, volunteer work, etc.

The first thing she advises is to turn off the TV (taking some comfort in the knowledge that it turns back on very easily). Don't allow the television to be the only mental exercise you do—it's simply too passive and ultimately not challenging on any level. "Even a thoughtful dinner party is a good way to exercise the mind. Invite some interesting people over whom you don't know well. Find out what inspires them. Choose a meal from another culture that you haven't tried cooking before. Challenge yourself and, in the process, get out of the chair and out of your rut. The current research is very clear—use it or lose it."

And Finally, Some Good, Home-Cooked Food for the Spirit

A lot of people view spirituality in the same way that they view going to religious services: as a weekly (or annual) ritual that has little or nothing to do with the rest of their lives. However, Rabbi Marc Gellman and Father Thomas Hartman, authors of the marvelous *The Dummies Guide to Religion*, remind us that while we're alive, the body and soul are inseparable. Thus, just as we must nourish and exercise the body for it to work efficiently, we must also feed and care for the soul. One without the other just won't cut it.

Of course, the standard way that we take care of our spiritual needs is to attend religious services and read the good books that have been guiding human behavior so presciently for thousands of years. If you haven't been to the church or temple or mosque in a while, you might be surprised at what you've been missing—and how hungry you are for the fullness of spirit that comes to so many simply by spending some quality time in a house of the Lord, listening to sermons, singing the ancient songs, hearing the eternal language of salvation.

However, as Interfaith Minister Dawn Deevy told me, going to religious services is not the only way to commune with God. She reminds us that a mindful walk in the woods can bring you right to the Creator's doorstep. Or, you can contemplate the entire universe through a kitchen window pane. Or, write down your thoughts so that others might share them. Or, read the profound thoughts of others—and take them to heart. It's good for your heart.

Ms. Deevy also suggests trying brief meditations or visualizations to enter that quiet inner sanctum: "Shakti Gawain's beautiful little book, *Creative Visualization*, provides simple and wonderful exercises that would help anyone achieve a measure of inner peace."

If all of that doesn't feel right to you—if you're not really a mediator or a church-goer or even a "deep" thinker—my suggestion is to borrow a page from Henri J. U. Nouwen's *The Wounded Healer*. Just as Jewish mystics knew thousands of years ago, the way to heal yourself (and incidentally the mystic's antidote for depression) is to help heal others. Volunteer at the children's hospital in your area or Amnesty International or just about any helping organization. You'll instantly feel better about yourself—and consequently you'll feel better.

Conclusion (But Not *The End*, As in...You Know What)

As a generation that's been to the moon and back—and along the way made a lot of rules and broken a lot of others—we have survived long enough to have gained at least a good, hearty taste of the wisdom of the ages. We are now the elders in our tribes. Decades ago we sang right along with Janis: "Freedom's just another word for nothing left to lose." Well, it still rings true today. Let's listen to ourselves. We're not free to do anything we choose. We need to take care of ourselves, body, mind, and spirit. We need to turn health into a verb. We need to be healthy (of body), wealthy (of mind), and wise (of spirit). We need to be ready for the everything that necessarily comes our way.

Translation: Get off your ass. Hop on that magic bus.

Chapter Six

Lost In the Health Care Bureaucracy

"…and you don't know what it is, do you, Mr. Jones?"
—Mr. Dylan

---

*C*autionary Tale 2: The Sequel:

Minor chest pains that woke me early one morning—and which did not go away three, four, five, six hours later—landed me flat on my back at one of our local emergency rooms, an annoying if perversely comforting beeping on the monitor hung precariously over my head.

Frankly, I didn't really think that I was having a heart attack—as a former EMT, a devoted watcher of medical television, and a cultural cousin of Woody Allen, I'm ridiculously well versed in the symptoms of a myocardial infarction. But I figured it would be downright adolescent of me to take any chances after six hours of chest pains at an age where all warranties have lapsed. I realized that Patti would be away for several more hours, so I put on some clean underwear (even in one's late fifties one must adhere to one's mother's advisories) and drove myself over to the hospital in nearby Poughkeepsie.

Noting the blood stains on the curtains pulled to protect my privacy while an EKG was recording electrical impulses in my burning heart, I never felt more unimportant in my whole life. Like a man desperately clinging by his fingertips to an elevator door that was closing, I made it a point to tell each of the several nice-enough technicians who peered inside, that I was not alone in the universe. Squeezing megabytes of information into those bloody curtains of opportunity, I let them know that I have seven kids. That I am a teacher. That I am a writer. That I coached kids' soccer. That I enjoy a good raunchy joke. That I actually have nicer clothes than I was wearing. That I don't always wear black briefs. That there are people who love me, who need me, *who would be by my side if only they knew where I was.*

Lying there like a walletless man in an alley, I fervently wished that Herb Weinman, our former family doctor, were still in practice. The truth is, I don't know if Herb was a great doctor (I didn't go to medical school). But if Herb were still around, I never would have taken off alone to the hospital. I would have called him. He would have known exactly what to say to ease my fears. And he would certainly have driven the five or six miles over to my house or arranged to meet me at his office in town.

Since Herb hung up his stethoscope quite a few years ago, I have not found a physician whom I trust to treat me as a friend. These days I go to various and nameless group practices, just like I take my Honda to a Jiffy-Lube. For my prostate, I see one of the three partners at a Poughkeepsie firm who doesn't remember me from yearly visit to yearly visit. For a recent sigmoid oscopy I engaged the services of a local doctor who has seen parts of me not even my wife would not recognize; I can't recall his name. For annual physicals, I check the updated list of providers provided by my insurance company so that I can have the whole thing done for $16 rather than $400. They don't know anything about me except what is scribbled on my charts. I see them glance quickly at the top of the folder to call me by name.

Some of the physicians I've encountered are good mechanics, some have nice deskside manners, some seem to listen to me when I recount symptoms, and for all that I know, some may even be much better diagnosticians than Herb. But none of them know me well enough—or want to know me well enough—to distinguish me from my symptoms—or my symptoms from somebody else's.

The emergency room brought that lonely truth to an artform. Left alone for fifteen or twenty minutes at a time over the course of two hours that felt more like two weeks of quarantine, I quickly tired of craning my neck and watching the running ticker tape of electrical impulses over my head. I became a detached observer of my own unremarkable treatment. The busy staff were not disrespectful or abusive. They were not incompetent. They were not callous in any way. They were, behind the practiced smiles and the calm voices, routinely indifferent.

I was as inert and inconsequential as an air filter in their rubber gloved hands. I was as I appeared on the computer screen: a series of parts, consequences, and outcomes. I was a case. A faceless client quickly filed and forgotten as soon as the next client was transferred to my stretcher.

In contrast, the elderly woman who was wheeled in on the gurney across the way was a real person. I gleaned from the muffled conversations that she had a local doctor who had already spoken to the E.R. staff. She also had a desperately worried, middle-aged son with a buttoned cardigan sweater and rubbber boots who was driving the nurses crazy with his questions about her labored breathing.

The nurses' calm and cool voices were warm and engaging when they told the woman and her son that Dr. B. would be in soon. The attending physician not only took vitals and queried her about the history of her condition, but asked how her Christmas had been. And when her doctor cruised in like a breath of Caribbean air—and called her Ruth and held her hand—she smiled as if she was on the chaise lounge to recovery. Her nervous son beamed.

Not me. I had a brief discussion with the attending doc who seemed understandably distracted and tired. He did his best to assure me that I was not having a heart attack, and even offered me a scrip for discomfort as a consolation prize for not getting the Big One, as Redd Foxx used to say. And, when he disappeared from my life forever, one of the nurses gave me two sheets of word-processed instructions—in case the symptoms persisted—and I was released in my own recognizance. As far as I knew, I was fine. Chestwall pain was the handy diagnosis, created I suppose to give a non-descript patient with a non-specific ailment a quasi-medical term to tell his family and friends. And, more to the point, to satisfy the insurance company. And, to get me on my way to make room for the fractured femur I heard called in on the crackling ambulance radio.

Of course I was relieved to find out that my ticker was still ticking away normally. Perhaps, finally, that is all that counts. But several years later, the pain squeezing through my heart has never quite gone away. It has only moved from my chestwall to a place deeper in the core of my body's being, a place undetectable by x rays and EKGs and MRIs. It is a dull ache, a fearful reminder that as our world grows less and less personal each day, the kind of unmanaged care that Herb Weinman once offered my family will soon be as obsolete and trivialized as a Norman Rockwell painting.

I know that the overworked staff who treated me at the emergency room that day were good and decent folk. But I also know that they did not take personal interest in my well-being. How could they? They did not know me. And, there was no one there who could speak for me as I would speak for myself—if I could not speak for myself. There was not a soul there who would have cried if I had died. Herb Weinman would have.

And I want that. I want that.

A Riff on New Age Health and Wellness

If you think that I'm now going to lay out the time transcendent process by which you might navigate the path back to your own good ol' home-visiting, feeling-your-pain, fatherly Doc Weinman, think again. It aint happening. It's over. Sorry. I mean, I'm really sorry. Apparently, this is not the glorious New Age of health and wellness that we once so hopefully envisioned from outside the commune.

Nevertheless, it is what it is—and in truth there are many aspects to this real new age that make the recent good old days of health care seem downright primitive, dogmatic, mechanistic, unhealthy, and even life-threatening. From the immensely (immensely, immensely) improved medical technology to the great advances in pharmaceuticals to the more humane and humanistic training of physicians, each of us is far more likely than ever in medical history to run into a doctor who treats the whole person…who at least is aware of alternative and complementary therapies…and who truly understands the principles behind preventive medicine and might even practice them in his or her own life.

That's the good news. As Cat Stevens once recommended smilingly, "… thinking about the good things to come"; don't discount those odd and unexpected gifts from the universe.

Yet, not one of us has to look too far down the medical chart to conclude that for the vast majority of us, medical care has grown as increasingly impersonal as it has grown disproportionately expensive. In a country or a culture that, for whatever reasons, does not support, believe in, or even aspire to universal health care, every single one has to get real about the two major medical issues for the New Millennium: personal responsibility and health insurance.

For those of us who are sixty, we need to get real about it all right away. Really.

Yes, Virginia, Good Things Happen to Bad People

You already know this—and in case you overlooked it, Rabbi Kushner wrote a not-to-miss book on the subject: *Bad Things Happen to Good People*. Indeed, with a nod and apologies to M. Scott Peck and a whole host of other visionaries, health is not fair. Bad things sometimes happen to good people who take very good care of themselves. Even more distressing, wantonly good health is sometimes visited upon some reprobates who smoke, eat poorly, scoff at exercise, and drink too much and too often. Thus the central question that will fuel the rest of your life after sixty: What does it actually mean to live well in a universe that doesn't play by the rules—and when your mommy and daddy are no longer running interference for you (as if...)?

So, we're not in Kansas anymore, Toto—and judging by the reactionary politics that define that state these days, that's probably a damn good thing. But we're also no longer in the good hands of folks like Dr. Marcus Welby or, closer to home, physicians like Herb Weinman who seemed to genuinely care about our well-being. We are on our own. You are on your own. And although good and decent and forward thinking post-60s physicians like Bernie Siegel and Andre Weill implore us to "love" our doctors as a means to best employ our mind's and body's resources for health, it's long past obvious for many of us (including the two dearly departed Beatles) that each of us needs a lot more than love to get and stay well.

As Sheldon Kopp wrote in his cautionary book, *If You Meet the Buddha on the Road, Kill Him!* gurus and blind faith are anathemas to health and self-actualization. At the risk of being dismissed as a terminal cynic, I suspect that the very last person in the universe that any of us want to trust blindly with our health is a physician. Just as you'd be a fool to trust even a trusty mechanic with a blank check to do a major overhaul of your rusty old VW Microbus, you'd have to have the mind of an acid head to offer up your body to anyone who has a world of other things on his or her mind. Mechanic or physician, minister or visionary, it is an unhealthy thing to put your faith in anyone other than yourself—or God. This is not alchemy or quantum physics—nor is it the 'ludes speaking: Everyone else on this good earth has a different set of priorities and goals that may or may not include you or your well-being. If we learned anything from Vietnam (which is questionable) or Altamont or the Chicago Seven, passivity and/or wishful thinking is no way to stop the machine or germs or evil. You, and sometimes only you, need to act on your own behalf.

In order to act in affirmative ways to guard your health, here are three simple things that each of us needs to be hip to:

• **The "Yadda Yadda Yadda, Blah Blah Blah, Yul Brynner Et Cetera, Et Cetera, Et Cetera, Everybody in the Universe Already Knows Everything You're Gonna Say and Almost No One Does It" Program.** Get a yearly physical, a bi-yearly colonoscopy, a mammogram every year, take some vitamins, exercise regularly, and eat a balanced diet. Don't treat your car better than you treat your body. Don't treat your cat or your plants better than yourself. Don't wait for Ed McMahon to arrive at your door with a check for 15 million dollars and a free health pass for life. Just do it.

• **Make nice with the Internet**. Honestly, after the life-affirming act of taking good care of yourself, this might well be the single most important tool for health maintenance after age 60. If you don't know how to use a computer, go out first thing tomorrow (after your raisin bran, coffee, and morning dump, of course) and buy yourself a cheap computer—and then, without stopping for lunch, sign up for a computer class at your local adult ed. facility or community college. Surfing the net for health information is the best and most effective way of researching medications, procedures, physicians, hospitals, etc. It's too complicated to do a decent job explaining how to research on the Internet here, but after your beginning course if you still don't know how to go about doing it, take another course. It's that important.

- **Do not take any medication, herb, potion or elixir just because your cousin Bernie swears it cured his piles**— or because Oprah promises it will change your life—or even because your doctor prescribed it for you. Check with your pharmacist. Surf the net. Find out what it really does.

- **Do not choose a doctor because she or he is "The Best" in the country/region/city according to your Aunt Sadie**, who is only slightly more reliable than Ellen de Generes, who is probably just as reliable as your doctor, who is passing and receiving referrals like they're notes in English 9 class and who is no more reliable than the patently unreliable yearly ratings in *New York Magazine*, which bases its recommendations on what??? (FYI, everybody in New York City sees the best doctor on the East Coast—just as everyone in LA sees the best doctor on the West Coast. All those best doctors, so little time.) Get a computer.

- **Avoid hospitals whenever possible**. From the staggering numbers of nosocomial (hospital borne) infections to the staggeringly overworked health care workers to the depressive atmosphere of a place full of sick and dying people, a hospital is the last place you'd want to be when you're sick or injured. Go to a hospital only when there's no other place to get well. And, get a computer.

- **However, if you get sick or injured and *must* go into the hospital, choose one with the lowest nosocomial and death rates** and arrange for a health advocate or two or three to be with you as much as possible to avoid things like overdoses, underdoses, wrong doses, someone else's doses, someone else's operation, or the right procedure on the wrong side of your body. (I teach several RNs who tell me they wouldn't even go into their own hospitals without someone to advocate for them—without someone to speak for them when they can't speak for themselves.) And finally, get a computer.

Insurances, Assurances, and Reassurances

As with your IRA or TIAA-Creff, you've got good health insurance by the time you get into your sixties or you don't. However, that's

not to say that it's too late to protect yourself against the kinds of catastrophic economic penalties that sometimes go along with your annual
physical or something far more serious.

I don't want to lose my house, my savings (har har—and you might
want to follow that up with a hardee har har har) or my ability to pur-
chase something better than dog food for my evening meal because I
owe some doctor or institution more money than I made cumulatively
over my working life to pay off an ordinary hernia operation.

I'm also not going to jive you by rewording the following section
and making it sound like it's coming from my pea-sized brain. I'm quot-
ing directly from the medicare.gov website. Know this information and
know it well:

> "The Centers for Medicare & Medicaid Services (CMS)
> administers Medicare, the nation's largest health insurance
> program, which covers nearly 40 million Americans. Medi-
> care is a Health Insurance Program for people 65 years of age
> and older, some disabled people under 65 years of age, and
> people with End-Stage Renal Disease (permanent kidney
> failure treated with dialysis or a transplant).

Again, Medicare is a health insurance program for:

- People 65 years of age and older.
- Some people with disabilities under age 65.
- People with End-Stage Renal Disease (permanent kidney failure
  requiring dialysis or a transplant).

Medicare has Two Parts:

- **Part A (Hospital Insurance)**

Most people do not have to pay for Part A.
- **Part B (Medical Insurance)**

Most people pay monthly for Part B.

That's it. If you want to know more, boot up the computer and go to www.medicare.gov. Everything you ever wanted to know about Medicare can be found there.

And when all is said and done, if you still need support check out:

National Senior Citizens Law Center
1330 Broadway, Suite 525
Oakland, CA 94612
510-663-1055
nsclc.org

Day Two: Sex, Drugs, and Rock & Roll (After the Early-Bird Special and Preferably Before Midnight)

Quill
Waitin' For You

Country Joe MacDonald
I Find Myself Missing You
Rockin' All Around The World
Flyin' High All Over The World
Seen A Rocket
Fish Cheer/I-Feel-Like-I'm-Fixing-To-Die-Rag

John Sebastian
How Have You Been
Rainbows All Over Your Blues
I Had A Dream
Darlin' Be Home Soon
Younger Generation

Keef Hartley Band
Believe In You
Rock Me Baby
Medley (from album Halfbreed)
. . . Leavin' Trunk
. . . Halfbreed
. . . Just To Cry
. . . And Sinnin' For You

Santana
Persuasion
Savor
Soul Sacrifice
Fried Neckbones

Incredible String Band
Catty Come
This Moment Is Different
When You Find Out Who You Are

Canned Heat
A Change Is Gonna Come/Leaving This Town
Woodstock Boogie
Going Up The Country
Let's Work Together
Too Many Drivers At The Wheel

Grateful Dead
St. Stephen
Mama Tried
Dark Star/High Time
Turn On Your Lovelight

Credence Clearwater Revival
Born On The Bayou
Green River
Ninety-Nine And A Half (Won't Do)
Commotion
Bootleg
Bad Moon Rising
Proud Mary
I Put A Spell On You
Night Time Is The Right Time

Keep On Choogin'
Suzy Q

Janis Joplin
Raise Your Hand
As Good As You've Been To This World
To Love Somebody
Summertime
Try (Just A Little Bit Harder)
Kosmic Blues
Can't Turn You Loose
Work Me Lord
Piece Of My Heart
Ball and Chain

Sly and the Family Stone
M'Lady
Sing A Simple Song
You Can Make It If You Try
Stand!
Love City
Dance To The Music
Music Lover
I Want To Take You Higher

The Who
Heaven And Hell
I Can't Explain
It's A Boy
1921
Amazing Journey
Sparks
Eyesight To The Blind
Cristmas
Tommie, Can You Hear Me
Acid Queen
Pinball Wizard
Abbie Hoffmann Incident
Fiddle About
There's A Doctor I've Found
Go To The Mirror, Boy
Smash The Mirror
I'm Free
Tommy's Holiday Camp
We're Not Gonna Take It
See Me, Feel Me
Summertime Blues
Shakin' All Over
My Generation
Naked Eye

Jefferson Airplane
The Other Side Of This Life
Plastic Fantastic Lover
Volunteers
Saturday Afternoon/Won't You Try
Eskimo Blue Day
Uncle Sam's Blues
Somebody To Love
White Rabbit

Chapter Seven

Sex and the Sexagenarian

"Let's Spend the Night Together" (or, as sung on the Ed Sullivan
Show, *"Let's Spend Some Time Together"*)
—The Rolling Stones, still rolling

/t's probably not a good idea to open a chapter on sex "in later life"
with the phrase "Remember when…," (or by singing along with the
Earls, "Re-mem-mem, re-mem-mem-mem-ber …"), but, as with so many
other topics related to reaching sixty, good or even reasonable suggestions are often irrelevant or boring when it comes to maintaining a rich,
hip, pulsing, pulsating existence.

So…throwing caution to the wind: Remember when any surface
without spikes—horizontal, vertical, inclined, disinclined, etc.—provided
an opportunity to "love the one you're with"—or better still, love the
one you love. (Actually, now that I think about it, there were a fair amount
of folks I knew back then that didn't consider spikes a deal breaker.)

A Short History of Sex in the Sixties
I ask you to recall those days only because it is important to remember that the sixties were sexy, simple as that. Please be assured that is
not the usual kind of macho bragging about the good old days that senior citizens have been doing since Adam and Eve turned thirty and
started bragging about the good old days in the Garden; any period defined by the innocent notion of free love is nothing but full of The Rascals' "Good Lovin'." Although the Stones' "Let's Spend the Night Together" sounds terribly tame in the new pornographic millennium, that
song crossed every puritanical boundary that our parents' generation had

constructed to separate us from each other—and did it with enough panache to make it exhilarating.

Thus, although we were not the originators of the term "free love" (check out the utopian socialist thinkers of the 1820s and 1830s and the anti-Comstock sex radicals of the 1890s and 1900s), we did put a more egalitarian edge to it and, in the process, gave extensive lip service (among other service) to the famous concept of the "zipless fuck" (see below to stir your memory).

> *The zipless fuck is…free of ulterior motives. There is no power game, the man is not "taking" and the woman is not "giving"…. No one is trying to prove anything or get anything out of anyone. The zipless fuck is the purest thing there is. And it is rarer than the unicorn. And I have never had one.*
> —Erica Mann Jong, *Fear of Flying*

Nor have I. I never even came close to such unfettered nirvana—all those previously mentioned messy and gooey feelings, y'know. Indeed, in retrospect, learning what I have learned about messy and gooey feelings over the years, I don't suppose many of us did. I do suppose, however, that we were greatly mistaken about the ways in which one might separate oneself from one's sexuality.

While it's probably true that every loving couple since Zeus and Hera were getting it on (or, if you prefer others, Cleopatra and Marc Antony or Liz Taylor and Richard Burton) and thinking that they invented beautiful sex, it's pretty clear that, for better and worse, Baby Boomers produced, directed, starred in, edited, spliced, provided culinary services for, and worked the boom on the Free Love movement, sixties style. I say better *and* worse because we are primarily responsible for the over-the-top sexualized everything sequel in which we are now living, and that includes Paris Hilton's surprisingly sexless home videos. (You can stop smirking now.)

After the cultural chastity belt that defined, refined, and undermined the fifties—when Lucy and Ricky were not even allowed by CBS censors to sleep in the same bed or mention that scurrilous word "pregnant"—and the great moral guide Ed Sullivan protected us from Elvis's gyrating hips and Mick's lewd suggestions to spending the night to-gether—our generation took sex out from behind closed doors, locked rooms, bathrooms, barn lofts, bordellos, boardwalks, dark movie the-aters, the back seats of Chevrolets, and, most important of all, the dankest recesses of the psyche crippled with guilt, repulsion, and self-contempt. With a little help from our friends, Masters and Johnson (and let's not forget the late great Alex Comfort), we paved the way for the American public to view the full-frontal of Elvis' gyrating pelvis and uncovered the great Puritan secret that had been kept in chains for several of hundred years: There is actually great joy to be found in sex…even without benefit of procreation.

As the great and late Marvin Gaye crooned before his father took him out, perhaps it was a case of "Sexual Healing" for the whole culture.

I Just Wanna Reach Out and, Uh, Bite Ya (Gene Vincent)

Of course there were excesses. All revolutions breed excess. Free Love, open marriage, and promiscuity run amok were not just fun and games, but also led to broken hearts, broken families, crabs, herpes, mi-sogyny and things far worse and far more perilous. And, while it may be hysterical at first to learn where various friends got it on back in the day, it quickly becomes pretty boring and adolescent. Like porn. Maybe even as boring as the "You should have seen how loaded I was at _____ (name your festival)" one-way conversation.

But for now there is no denying how invigorating, elevating, giddy-ing, and sexy it was to be in the throes of a cultural revolution where young people, already driven by their hormones and their ideals, were no longer ashamed of their bodies.

The Pill Versus the Springhill Mining Disaster and Other Great Riffs

Some quick history on the evolution of the modern sexual revolu-tion: With the introduction of the birth control pill (first marketed as we were entering puberty in 1960), the worldwide ignorance of AIDS, and the vast, vast, vast misimpression that penicillin would cure every other STD known to human kind, we were set free to hump 'til the cows or our parents came home, whichever came first. And at the humping heart of the whole thing was The Pill, perhaps the most socially significant medical advance of the century. By 1962, approximately 1.2 million American women were using it; and by 1965, 5 million; and by 1973, about 10 million.

Simply, the pill changed everything. And with all due respect to Timothy Leary, it was far more powerful than an acid tab.

So much for the historical perspective. We didn't invent sex, but as a generation we certainly did our best to give it a good name.

From Fred Neil: Everybody's Talking At Me, Can't Hear a Word They're Sayin'

There is a "wealth" of advice out there in the bookstores and on the web about enjoying senior sex. But after all these decades of perfecting or at least duplicating your own version of the horizontal mambo, what don't you know? Despite the culture's overwhelming preoccupation with sex, sex is not neurosurgery or quantum physics. It's pretty much a three parter: 1) With clean hands or tongue gently inspect all relevant parts to make sure they're lubed and ready to go; 2) Insert Part A into Part B (or C or D); and 3) As Bob Marley would say, begin "… jammin' in the name of the Lord."

Nevertheless, there are now as many articles and books on senior sex as there are senior cats prowling around senior chicks in Palm Beach County looking to get it on. And they all pretty much say the same thing. But the good ones can be very helpful and the bad ones are just plain common knowledge. So I'm not going to add an echo to the good ones or add any more stupidity to the universe. However, I am going to make a recommendation (and in doing so offer some support for my good publisher): If you're looking for a substantive guide to sexual hijinks for seniors, the best book I've seen on the market is *Dr Ruth's Sex After 50: Revving Up the Romance, Passion & Excitement* by the famous Dr. Ruth Westheimer.

That Was Then, This Is Now:

The assumption that when you retire from your job, you also retire from your sexual life is a bogus vestige of the puritanical pretensions of the Greatest Generation and the Plymouth Rockers who begot them. It is also bogus, however, to think that sixty-year olds could or should be the sexual Olympians we were back in the sixties. Please.

To wit, the following compilation of headlines thirty-six years after Woodstock (gathered from SeniorJournal.com):

• *Eighty-two percent of Baby Boomer women are very or somewhat confident sexually.*

• *A sexy movie about senior citizens, what will they think of next?* (The movie is titled *The Other Side of the Street* and was made in Brazil, starring Academy Award nominated Fernanda Montenegro.)

• *Americans consider women over 50 just as beautiful as women under 30.* (From *Allure Magazine*'s article "The Allure of Beauty Study": When asked to name "the most beautiful person alive today," respondents named women between the ages of 50 and 70.)

• *Old Broads Get Naked for Charity Calendar* ("A Celebration of Mature Women").

• *Latest Senior Nudie Calendar Features Women 75 to 94* (seventeen ladies from the Atwood (MA) Senior Housing Center).

• *"Mild Bunch" Beefcake Biker Calendar Raises Funds for New Senior Center* (Old geezers from the Texas Hill Country to do a nude motorcycle calendar to raise funds for a senior citizens center.)

But Where Have All the Hormones Gone?

A bad joke here may be instructive or at least enable me to move the conversation along:

The Three Stages of Sex in Relationships

1. You make love anywhere, anytime, in every position imaginable.

2. You make love on weekend nights, behind closed doors, in the missionary position.

3. You pass in the hall and say "F— you!"

And with that, enough of the senior citizen sex jokes—you've no doubt heard them all—and probably told more than your share. So....

Just as your pecs and your gluts and few other pieces of that old stalwart hippie anatomy have dropped a notch or two over the years (and in some cases spread out as to provide a more comforting drop into a wooden chair), so naturally has your libido. (If it hasn't, you need to go to a doctor.) As Paul Simon once crooned, "… the nearer your destination, the more you're slip-sliding away." And just as our decreasing hormone levels have given way to neural synapses that better enable us to consider the implications of our actions, reliable statistics suggest that by age sixty very few of us are sleeping around indiscriminately—and fewer still consider airplane lavatories and elevators and speeding cars appropriate places to make love or just get it on. So, with apologies to Robert Zimmerman, while it's not quite "all over now, Baby Blue," the plane has landed and those of us who are still shakin' are in for a long taxi ride to the terminal. Why not enjoy ourselves en route?

So Let's Get the Big Problems Out of Way Right Away: Drum Roll....

Erectile Dysfunction

Always sounds a bit to me like a faulty erector set. Anyway, the term "erectile dysfunction" can mean the inability to achieve erection, an inconsistent ability to do so, or the ability to achieve only brief erections. As such, estimating the incidence of erectile dysfunction is very difficult. That said, according to the National Institutes of Health, in 2002, an estimated fifteen million to thirty million men in the United States experienced chronic erectile dysfunction. According to a National Ambulatory Medical Care Survey, approximately 22 out of every 1000 men in the United States seek medical attention for ED.

Also, as you might imagine, incidence of the disorder increases with age. Chronic ED affects about 5 percent of men in their forties and 15 percent to 25 percent of men by the age of sixty-five. Transient ED and inadequate erection affect as many as 50 percent of men between the ages of forty and seventy. Or getting hard is getting harder to do.

More: Diseases (e.g., diabetes, kidney disease, alcoholism, atherosclerosis) account for as many as 70 percent of chronic ED cases and psychological factors (e.g., stress, anxiety, depression) may account for 10 percent to 20 percent of all cases. Between 35 percent and 50 percent of men with diabetes experience ED. It's a big problem.

Female Sexual Dysfunction

Although the news media would have us believe that problems related to sexual functioning are exclusively male, it's simply not so. About ten million women between the ages of fifty and seventy-four report sexual problems. According to the researchers, the primary culprits may be a decreased sensation in the clitoris and vaginal dryness, which affect almost half of those in their study. It's also a real problem.

Solutions and Non-Solutions

If any of this sounds like you, go see your urologist/gynecologist. Don't go to a general practitioner. Don't self-medicate and buy pills over the Internet (see Chapter 10). Don't self-herbalate or overdose on zinc at the health food store. Don't buy a book about increasing your aging libido. Don't assume it's all in your head and run off to a shrink for twelve (more costly than you think) sessions about how you still want to sleep with Mom or Dad. Go see a urologist or gynecologist who knows what she or he is talking about when she or he is talking about sexual function. Then if you get no relief, go herbalate or rent some porn or make an appointment to talk about it with your local sex therapist.

The Good News

Viagra is the miraculous answer to the dirty little question that very few men once asked for fear of being outed. But by the time that Senator Bob Dole and baseball star Raphael Palmiero started shilling for Pfizer, and Jay Leno and David Letterman made the flaccid penis joke an acceptable part of late night jabber, the problem was resolved by a simple visit to the doctor (who, if over fifty, one could reasonably be assured was a Viagra user himself—or married to one).

A Brief History of the Artificial Boner

Sildenafil (or compound UK-92,480) was synthesized by a group of Pfizer chemists developing substances to relieve hypertension (high blood pressure) and angina pectoris (restriction of the cardiac arteries).

Clinical studies determined that the drug had little effect on angina, but it could induce marked penile erections. (I would have loved to have been around the lab when they figured that one out!) Not known for being dummies, the hoohas at Pfizer quickly decided to market it as a cure for erectile dysfunction. The drug was patented in 1996, and approved for use in erectile dysfunction by the Food and Drug Administration on March 27, 1998, becoming the first pill approved to treat erectile dysfunction in the United States. Levitra (vardenafil) and Cialis (tadalafil) quickly followed in its wake but the sale of Viagra alone from 199 to 2001 exceeded one billion dollars.

A 2005 study of senior citizen and Baby Boomer couples found that the sexual function and satisfaction of the females significantly improved after the erectile dysfunctional men in their lives were effectively treated for their problem. Well, duh!

The Not-So Good News

The good news, pretty much like all good news or simple pleasures, is complicated by some bad news that seems to always go along with it. So it is with Viagra. You shouldn't use this medicine if you take any of these forms of nitroglycerin or any other nitrates:

- Isosorbide mononitrate (brand names: Ismo, Monoket, Imdur)
- Isosorbide dinitrate (brand names: Isordil, Sorbitrate)
- Sublingual nitroglycerin tablets or spray (brand names: Nitrostat, Nitrolingual Spray)
- Transdermal nitroglycerin patches or paste (brand names: Minitran, Nitro-Dur, Transderm-Nitro)

You also shouldn't take sildenafil if you are taking other medicines for erectile dysfunction. Read the section on Sex and Death in Chapter 8.

And here's an eye opener: A small number of men have lost eyesight in one eye some time after taking Viagra, Cialis, or Levitra. This type of vision loss is called non-arteritic anterior ischemic optic neuropathy (NAION). NAION causes a sudden loss of eyesight because blood flow is blocked to the optic nerve. At this point it appears that men who have a higher chance for NAION include those who:

- have heart disease
- are over 50 years of age
- have diabetes
- have high blood pressure
- have high cholesterol
- smoke
- have certain eye problems

Last word: Don't go this alone. Speak to your doctor. Speak to your lover. Get to know your good sexy self.

Chapter Eight

Still Getting it On
After All These Years

or
Sex and Dislocation
or
Sex and Death
aka
The Kama Sutra vs. The Calmer Sutra

*T*itle of a recent AP news piece: *"Aging Baby Boomers Groan After Years of Exercise"*

The brief capsule behind the headline: "Sports injuries among Baby Boomers increased by 33 percent from 1991–1998, according to figures cited in a U.S. Consumer Product Safety Commission report. Baby boomers in 1998 suffered more than 1 million sports injuries, to the tune of nearly $19 billion in medical costs...."

In the nearly ten years since that study it hasn't gotten any better.

The Bong Half-Full

Here's the bong half-full interpretation: As a generation we're still remarkably active and, even more remarkably so, still playing the games we played forty years ago—in between partying and stints on the protest line. Just pick up the reading glasses hanging on your chest and take a look at the sports pages or crank up the high-def television: Older cats and chicks are still lighting up the scoreboard.

We're still running road races, going mountain biking, pounding the bag, jumping into scrums, lacing up the in-line skates, faking left and going hard to the hoop.

The Bong Half-Empty

The bong half-empty view: Judging by vast number of debilitating sports injuries in that Consumer Product Safety Commission report, we're evidently too old to be playing the same games in the same ways we did when we were in our twenties. Even more troubling, the consequences are cumulative.

As such, it's only going to get worse. And hurt more. And ultimately, it's going to kill us.

Throw the Bong Against the Fireplace

It is what it is. Bike, jog, smoke, drink, make love, and be merry, for tomorrow we die. We never listened well to authorities anyway; let's not start now. Generationally speaking, we do not act our age, which is both a very good thing and something to be very wary about. Okay, point made. Now, you ask, what the hell do sports injuries have to do with making love, not war?

Well, despite the fateful demise of the biological imperative (no more eggs, old geezer sperm doing the backstroke or dead man's float), great sex is the same as it always was, great, which means that it entails strenuous exercise.

Separate out all those gooey feelings that we all should have learned long ago cannot be separated from the act, and it's about physiology. It's about sweating, groaning, huffing and puffing. It's about muscle, bone, tendon, and blood coursing through stretched, atherosclerotic veins. For some us whose longest walk of the day is from the front door to the garage, it's the only exercise we get. Plus, ask anyone—especially men the morning after a misfire or a dud—and they'll tell you it's all about performance.

So it's a sport. And a lot of us are still playing.

Full Frontal Sport

Sex is a full-contact sport, complete with grimacing, dirty words, strategy, penetration, thrusting, parrying, goals, and conquest. And like all sports, one needs to stay in shape for sex. One must understand how to "get up" for the game—and how to avoid injury—and, just to make sure I'm covering all bases, how to avoid death. Injuries may be acceptable, but dying is clearly a very big a price for a few minutes of sensual pleasure.

Sex and Death I: It's a Guy Thing

As this brief section is primarily about men dying in the act, you older hipster women might just lie back and appreciate the scenery—and en route be made aware of the dangers from above. Although older women may actually die in the hours before or after sex (anticipation, boredom, annoyance, frustration?), the statistics are quite clear: Men kick off in record numbers during the act itself, right in the sack, face-in-bosom as it were.

Perhaps you recall former Governor of New York and former vice-president of the United States Nelson Rockefeller famously dropping off this mortal coil and into the eternally loving arms of his paramour, Megan Marshak? But there have been many, many, many (many) more whose last gasp came right along with an orgasm. A certain amount of respect and civility requires that I not name additional famous names, but let's be clear, randy old Nelson is not alone on the list. There is even a long and scurrilous history of Catholic popes who supposedly died during sex: Leo VII (936–9) died of a heart attack, John VII (955–64) was bludgeoned to death by the husband of the woman he was with at the time, John XIII (965–72) was also murdered by a jealous husband, Pope Paul II (1467–71) allegedly died while being sodomized by a page boy.

More troubling to practitioners of lifelong fidelity, University of Michigan researchers have reported that the male quest for sex wears out men long before their female counterparts. Just name a country—any country—and you can pretty much count on its women living longer than men. And this isn't a recent trend; it apparently has roots in our deep evolutionary history. From the extreme sexual display of male field crickets to present day Rambos in their Hummers, males of all species at all times have been aggressively competing for female affection. The result is a significant shortening of our lifespan relative to women. Put that in your pipe and don't smoke it.

Sex and Death II: It's Another Guy Thing

Here's a fact that should raise the raise the hairs on the necks of all men—and lift the eyebrows of all women:

In an article titled "Unfaithful Men More Likely to Die During Sex," the German magazine *Bild der Wissenschaft* reports that researchers at the Centre for Forensic Medicine studied nearly 30,000 post-mortem cases and found fifty-six instances of men who died of heart attacks during sex. Not a particularly shocking number given the physical exertion required during sex, right? But here's the kicker: Only one in four died in the arms of his wife or partner. The study found that *"More than half of them lived their last hour in the arms of a lover or at the brothel."* Worse still, *"The remainder died in the act of masturbation."*

The researchers could only speculate on why a disproportionate number died with lovers than with partners, suggesting that it may be because they were putting extra strain on their system by trying harder. I have to say that this begs the unasked question: Who are the overachieving masturbators and just who are they trying to impress? And I have to add, man, that's one ignominious way to check out!

Sex and Death III: Sex, Drugs, and If You Have an Erection for More than Four Hours, Go to an Emergency Room

Enough said.

Sex and Death IV: Listen Up, Babe

Although one could say with some confidence that sex isn't generally a spectator sport, let's be clear that there are many senior citizen orgies going on as I type—and you read—and there's a massive pornography industry in this country raising the heart rate and blood pressure of senior citizens from New York to Tokyo and from Iceland to Patagonia. Don't be shocked.

However, don't assume that I am condemning post-sixty pornography or group sex just because I find it generally unappealing, if not appallingly juvenile. If little else, we're old enough to know better. However, here are some more than interesting facts to consider before you jump into the senior mosh pit or take that hunka hunka senior burnin' love home for a one-night stand:

A 2004 CBS News report found that nearly 27 percent of people living with AIDS in America were fifty or older. The report focused on ordinary people like one woman who, at seventy-three, is the new, more mature face of AIDS. She contracted HIV from her boyfriend when she was fifty-six.

During the last decade, AIDS cases among the over-fifty crowd have soared from 16,000 in 1995 to 90,000 in 2003—a 500 percent increase. From CNN: Through 2002, the latest year for which statistics are available, 12,868 persons sixty-five and older have been diagnosed with AIDS. And from the *Palm Beach Post*: In 2002, the West Palm Beach to Boca Raton area ranked fifth in the nation for its rate of AIDS cases per 100,000 people.

Many AIDS activists say that due to Viagra and similar drugs, older Americans are, sexually active like never before. The new old joke among retirees is that if a man has a driver's license and a prescription, he's got himself a harem. Guys like that are called "Condo Cowboys."

First Time—Long Time, or Long Time—Long Time

So, whether you're a card carrying member of the Walt Chamberlain-Heidi Fleiss Society (you've been in and out, of the sack more times than you remember) or you've been playing sexual air hoops in your own private cat house since you were thirteen, don't underestimate the dangers of the pleasures that have followed us back to the future.

Expect Expectations

With all the history and incumbent anxieties of the Free Love Movement tucked neatly beneath the sexagenarian belt, there are also very (very) few of us in the surviving universe who are so comfortable with our sexuality that we are aren't even modestly daunted by the huge expectations (male, female, spice channel) for us to perform essentially superhuman miracles in bed.

The current ubiquitous buzz about Olympian-sized orgasms and tests and performance is not only intimidating, it's very destructive to real sex between real lovers of any age. Or so says Cynthia G. Pizzulli, Ph.D., an AASECT (American Association of Sex Educators, Counselors and Teachers) Certified Sex Therapist, from East Northport, New York. In our interview, Dr. Pizzulli suggested that far too many couples—experienced in sexual love or not—young or old—approach sex as a test to see whether their relationship is worthy. She says that there is far too much emphasis on "big bang sex," which is an "accident waiting to happen."

When the fireworks don't light up the entire sky, she says "… the larger than life expectation of sex becomes a negative fulfilling prophecy of your own sexual inadequacy." Translated, that means that the bigger the expectations for the night, the less likely you're going to truly enjoy the sex. It's going to feel like a performance. Or worse still, it will feel like a chore.

Sex Toys, Aphrodisiacs, Step-By-Step Instructions

Only kidding, I'm not going there. But you're not alone in hoping that this chapter—or any chapter anywhere—is somehow going to provide you with the kind of information that will not only enable you to attain sexual ecstasy, but will also establish you as the best ancient lover on the face of the earth. Definitely not alone.

So don't be surprised—maybe just disappointed—when Dr. Pizzulli (or any other reputable sex therapist) assures you for the umpteenth time in your long life that there are no sex toys, no aphrodisiacs, no secret primitive techniques and no step-by-step instructions that will allow you to fulfill all your fantasies of loving and being loved. Consider the cover of practically every magazine aimed at men and women in their twenties and thirties (and now forties): Each issue contains an article that identifies the three, seven, ten, whatever number of techniques guaranteed to bring you or your lover to the height of orgasmic ecstasy at will. Now think about it: If any of those techniques actually worked—at all—everyone would be completely satisfied and we'd never see another magazine cover promising to "Drive him/her crazy in bed." Yet we do see those covers, week after week after week. They're not evil. They're not bad. They just don't work. It's all smoke and mirrors (and not the kind that are on the ceiling).

What Really Leads to Erotic Connections

Dr. Pizzulli, who has been counseling couples for more than fifteen years on healthy, satisfying sexual relationships, says that there's far too much emphasis in this culture on technique and sexual aids—and far too little on the real communication that leads to erotic connections.

So leave the gymnastic positions and sex toys and aids for the next generation who will be less concerned with battery failure or dislocation of limbs. "Just talk," she says, "about anything. You'll find that the intimacy of the night itself will take over."

Talk the Talk

Ask any woman of any age about what turns her on and, among the hundred other things she might think of, she will tell you she wants to talk to her lover before making love. That doesn't mean making stilted conversation for five minutes before you start putting on the moves. In fact, Pizzulli suggests, it's the talk that occurs before the *big* night that really pays off in the bedroom.

And if talking mano a womano is too daunting, try some therapy sessions. Couples' therapy alone can be a wonderful form of foreplay; practically everybody gets aroused just talking about sex.

Pizzulli adds that although most men are comfortable telling their lovers what they want and like in bed, they are generally uncomfortable discussing their sexual desires—much less their sexual anxieties—outside the bedroom. Yet the reality is that talking openly with one's partner is not only a good way to deactivate fear of failure but an entirely erotic thing to do. As almost anyone involved in the business of sex will tell you, the single most erotic organ in the body is the mind—and I would like to add that the mouth (and we're not talking oral sex—it's more like aural sex) is literally the voice of the mind.

Troubleshooting (or Trouble Shooting)

Whatever the problem you might have in bed (use your imagination), it's really up to you whether you turn it into a cancerous symbol of things to come or a great private joke between the two of you. At our age we should know how beautifully human each of us can be—and laugh about it. Indeed, there is an intimacy that comes with laughter between naked souls that is as sexy as it comes.

Dr. Marj Steinfeld, a family therapist from northern New Jersey who you will hear from again in Chapter 9, has written extensively on the healing effects of laughter and good humor, and I couldn't agree more. At the heart of laughter is the acknowledgement that we're all human—we're all bozos on the same bus. There are no superheroes in bed, just two people who love each other enough to lose themselves in each other's pleasure.

She reminds Boomers that sex is not only supposed to be fun, it is fun. Don't make it a battleground. Don't make it a contest. Don't bring anyone else into it. "It's the one wonderfully private connection between two people that never ever has to go anywhere else except between the two of you."

Above all, enjoy each other. Bring each other pleasure. That's what it's all about anyway. Right?

Sex and Dislocations, Sprains, and Strains: (Pssst, if you Groan While Tieing Your Shoes, This Is a Very Important Section to Read)

The point of all this is that while sex may be an important part of a healthy, happy later life (it also may not be important—more on that later), it's pretty clear that good sex serves some different purposes than it did when we were younger. And the more adolescent and narcissistic aspects of physical love, e.g., mirrors, pole dancing, dick tricks, dirty talking, etc., may no longer serve as the effective arousal tools that they once did.

Along the same lines, there are many Kama Sutra positions that should have warning labels: NOT FOR MATURE ADULTS or "The Surgeon General Generally Warns Against People Fifty and Over Trying This Position."

If you can stand it, another quick history: The Indian guide to sexual love, the *Kama Sutra*, was supposedly written by Vatsyayana Mallanaga in or around the third century BC. The text is originally known as *Vatsyayana Kamasutram* ("Vatsyayana's Aphorisms on Love"). Very little is known about Vatsyayana, but it's clear that the *Kama Sutra* is not even the first Indian sex guide. Vatsyayana himself mentions several sages who trod the erotic path before him. The Chinese had sex manuals 500 years earlier, and Ovid's "Ars Amatoria," a handbook for courtesans, preceded the *Kama Sutra* by some 200 years.

An interesting sidebar: According to some researchers, the *Kama Sutra*'s author was a celibate scholar. Celibate scholar or not, Vatsyayana had a wildly erotic imagination. He believed there were eight ways of making love, multiplied by eight positions within each of these. As such, there are 64 "Atrs" in total.

The sexual culture the *Kama Sutra* describes is also surprisingly like our own, or at least 1960 something to 1980 something. But—need I remind you?—we are very much unlike the movin' and groovin' boys and girls we were back in famous '69, and, conservatively speaking, there should be Surgeon General Warnings on at least sixty of the sixty-four Atrs to protect us from chronic, debilitating injury practically guaranteed to put us in crutches or wheelchairs for the rest of our lives.

Here are eight Kama Sutra positions that should never be tried by anyone over fifty:

1. **The Amazon**—The man lies down on his back with the legs slightly opened and flexed towards his chest. "The amazon is the woman who rides her man of (sic) the wildest and primitive way." *No!* Just imagine the forced flatulence and potential for dislocations, fractures, slipped discs, and the consequent PTSD that follows you out of the emergency room.

2. **The Armchair**—This position is a variant of the Amazon, where the woman's bent knees rest over her lover's shoulders and both partners are leaning back at a forty-five degree angle. Add paralysis to the list potential complications of The Amazon. As Ralph Nader might say, this position may be unsafe at any age.

3. **The Hammock**—The man is seated with his legs flexed…oh, forget the description, the name itself should be a warning.

4. **The Fusion**—As above. All I need to add about this is that you risk being fused for the rest of your natural life—and may even have to be buried together.

5. **The Mill Vanes**—He's on top of her facing one direction, she's on the bottom facing the other direction, his feet near her face, her feet near his face. As Kurtz uttered as he peered into the Heart of Darkness, "The horror! The horror!"

6. **The Trapeze**—Frankly, I couldn't follow the Indian translation (or the illustration), so I turned to the description I found in *Cosmopolitan* magazine: "… place the backs of your knees in the crooks of his elbows and pull upward so that your lower back and butt are raised off the bed at a 20 to 30 degree angle and the backs of your thighs are pressed against his stomach and chest…." Got the picture? Erase it immediately. I suspect you could do damage to yourself merely by dreaming about this position.

7. **The Wheel Barrow**—A variation of the old wheel barrow races we ran as children. The only question here is whether the climax involves her broken and bruised nose or his bilateral shoulder dislocation. Time to grow up. A quote from W. B. Yeats might help: "That is no country for old men. The young/ In one another's arms…Caught in that sensual music all neglect/ Monuments of unageing intellect." Or from the Doors: "Dont you love her as she's walkin' out the door."

8. **The Variant of Medusa**—This position is described as one for men "equipped with flexibility and resistance." That's your first clue that there should be an ambulance in the driveway waiting to transport you to the hospital when it's all over. Then it goes on to say something about "Squatting…." Squatting? Men over sixty don't squat and get up again. Keep in mind that Medusa was a Greek Mythological figure (big eyes, fangs, brass hands, hair of writhing snakes) who could turn anyone who looked upon her into stone. That's you, mister, unable to ever move again.

What's Left?

You know what's left. From Jim Morrison, "Love me two times":

1. **The Good Ol' Fashioned All-American Missionary Position**—classic and universal, but not for that reason boring. The face-to-face allows a infinity of variants to make it more attractive and exciting. The mobility of the hands, the proximity of the faces and the comfort of the bodies are the advantages that made it famous. It is a position that many identify with love and romance, the beginnings of a pair, the adolescence. As my Uncle Murray would reason: Who could argue with that?

2. **The Woman on Top**—a nice variant of the traditional Missionary position. Saves her from being crushed. And, makes that big belly thing much less of a problem. Gives her greater pressure—and pleasure. From Uncle Murray's lifelong squeeze, Aunt Betty: Who could argue with that?

Five Easy Pieces

So there are at least five things to consider up front (or behind if that's your thing):

• **Good sixties sex involves a little humility.**—This, in essence, is the simple unabashed acknowledgement of physical reality. At sixty we simply can't surf, rock climb, trek, run, eat, drink, hump, dump, bump (and grind), or pump it up like we once did. Despite Mick's amazing cavorting on stage (looking more and more each day like the Grateful Dead's dangling skeleton than the rocker he used to be), and despite the fact that we are, to our everlasting unquenchable pride, a most un-humble generation, if we've learned little else from arriving at age sixty, life is a remarkable leveler. No one—no one—gets to this stage of life with being profoundly humbled. If you don't know that, you've been high for far too long—it's not good karma.

• **More is not better**. Less is not better. Better is better. What's the big difference between making love once a day or once a week or once a month? If you're making love with someone you care about and you're doing it as often, or infrequently, as feels right, who gives a crap (though I should add that once a year is not nearly enough). In fact, all that lost sexual energy could be put to creative activities that may sustain you longer than any 45-second orgasm.

• **There are no aphrodisiacs**. Sorry. Much like the Spanish Fly rumors of our youth and the banana smoking of our late adolescence, aphrodisiacs are fictions created by people who lack the imagination and the eternal presence of mind to see pleasure for what it is. Despite reports of the development of a sexual enhancement drug PT-141—which has been hyped as being a powerful sexual enhancer for women, "the aphrodisiac of the 21st Century"—it is "still being tested." That is, it is another figment of another horny, unimaginative man's imagination, which includes blow up dolls.

• **There is no such thing as a sexual performance enhancer**. Sorry again. Don't be tempted by Zimaxx, Libidus,

Neophase, Nasutra, Vigor-25, Actra-Rx or Yilishen and 4EVERON, products marketed for erectile dysfunction and enhancing sexual performance. The FDA put the "beware label" on seven of these types of products, saying "they are in fact illegal drugs that contain potentially harmful undeclared ingredients."

> • **Penis enlargement is for fools (or as my kids say, dickheads)**. Think with your head instead of other parts of your anatomy. Love the thing you're with.

Advice from a Yogi: It's Not Over 'til It's Over

Now that we've dispensed with all the warnings, imagine the sound of the other shoe falling right before the swish of socks and underwear: Of course, it's not over. Sex and sexiness doesn't just disappear with the hair and the flat tummies and the tight neck. Despite the utter repulsion with which the present teens and twenty-somethings regard their elders having sex, every study from every corner of the globe supports the notion that sexual function for most people goes on into and through their dotage. (Now with Viagra and Cialis and the like, we're probably good to go right up to and through deep coma—something like nurse Jenny in *The World According to Garth*.) We just don't ratchet it up that often—and, like the joke regarding stage two, it's mostly on soft horizontal surfaces, behind closed doors.

As Gail Sheehy said, "With each passage of human growth we must shed a protective structure like a hardy crustacean. We are left exposed and vulnerable—but also yeasty and embryonic again, capable of stretching in ways we hadn't known before."

If it didn't sound so stupid and retro, I'd say "Right on, Babe!"

Chapter Nine

Roommates/Housemates/ Shacking Up/Living in Sin

Shacking up is all you want to do
—Fleetwood Mac

*I*n those days when the notion of being sixty was nothing more than a hallucination for a whole generation of Peter Pans, Patti and I would occasionally fantasize about someday buying a gigantic Victorian house somewhere warm and balmy (big veranda, live oaks, weeping willows, a long green lawn sloping down to a long dock through the reeds to some quiet body of water…and in our old(er) age (of course we'd all still look and feel like we're 25), we'd answer all those questions about reduced incomes and diminished energy by sharing that paradise with our closest friends and/or Patti's sister Leigh and her husband George— and, of course, maintain a small *pied-a-terre* in Greenwich Village when we needed to get away or wanted to hear some live music. The new and improved New Age commune for the Sixties

Not a bad idea actually, but now that the merry-go-round-the decade has passed the smirking toothless operator a few more times, the truth is that the last thing I want to do is live with anyone but my wife. And that includes living with my grown kids—in my house or, worse, theirs. Just as the great dream of communal living pretty much passed out of mind and sight along with Spiro Agnew, these days I look forward to friends and family coming over for the night or the weekend and then look forward to closing the door and watching their cars disappear down the long driveway and out through the woods.

My home, to quote the nineteenth entury English pastor Frederick

William Robertson (1816–1853)—who missed 60 by twenty-three years—has become "… the one place in all this world where hearts are sure of each other. It is the place of confidence. It is the place where we tear off that mask of guarded and suspicious coldness which the world forces us to wear in self-defense, and where we pour out the unreserved communications of full and confiding hearts. It is the spot where expressions of tenderness gush out without any sensation of awkwardness and without any dread of ridicule."

That's a hard place to find if you don't know each other inside and out for a lot of decades.

The problem for many of us is that old existential thang about an unpredictable universe. By sixty most of the assumptions we lived by at twenty or thirty have fallen away, along with the hair and the breasts at the top of our chests. A lot of us are separated, divorced, widowed…and alone. By seventy those numbers go up exponentially. And by then loneliness is one of the real challenges for old hippies.

In the January 2006 issue of the *Journals of Gerontology: Psychological Sciences*, it was reported that the types of social networks older adults maintain are related to their mental health. Based on a sample of 1,669 U.S. adults aged 60 and older, surveyed as part of the ISR Americans' Changing Lives study, the researchers found that friendships were more important than family relationships in predicting good mental health. Apparently, many seniors want friends and confidantes more than they want marriage partners

Around the same time, the *New York Times* ran a feature on a senior citizen version of MTV's "Real World" located in central New Jersey. The residents of this "commune," who range in age from sixty-five to eighty, share space for many of the same reasons so many of us lived together in the sixties and seventies—money, friendship, emotional support, shared vision, and shared responsibilities. The housemates are not related by blood or marriage and they do not necessarily share the same tastes, politics, or schedules. They are simply "fond enough" of each other to manage expenses by sharing space—and, in the process, ward off debilitating loneliness.

Just the Facts, Ma'am

During the last 25 years, according to the AARP, the number of people living in "nontraditional" households—without relatives or romantic partners—has grown steadily. The U.S. Census Bureau reports the number of senior citizens cohabitating without getting married has doubled in the past decade. Various experts say this is a trend likely to increase as the Baby Boom generation gets older.

In this most intriguing confluence of cultures, in which grandparents and grandchildren are living similar lifestyles, it turns out that some 4.7 million were unmarried twosomes in 2000, up about 62 percent from 1990 and nearly three times the number from 1980. Some demographers think the numbers are actually much higher, since a good number of couples are reluctant to report their living arrangements.

Living in Sin

Back in the day when the term "living in sin" was actually considered sinful, my friends and I in Madison, Wisconsin—your friends and you wherever you were—had already been shacking up since everyone got out of the freshman dorms.

In those early days of the supposed sexual revolution, practically everybody messed around as freshmen, but at the end of the night, which was often the next morning, you went back to your own messy dorm room with your own messy and smelly roommate. During the sophomore year, though, when almost everybody either got an apartment or dropped out of school and mainstream life altogether, it made sense to have roommates—and it made even more sense to have a bedmates. Thus, living in sin became de rigeur—and thus no longer sinful.

We were playing house. Really playing house because my parents and others provided so little modeling of the kind of domestic intimacies that we imagined when we closed our eyes and thought about the kind of love that would last a lifetime. And it seemed as if everyone was in on the game—or at least not interested in tipping over the board.

In 1968, Patti's mother, who clearly suspected her daughter was shacking up with me, would call her apartment at the oddest hours, ostensibly to trap her into a blubbering confession and rediscovered chastity. But when her daughter wasn't home at 6 A.M. on a Saturday morning—or midnight Wednesday—she would either accept the ridiculous excuse that she slept over a friend's apartment or provide the answer herself: "I tried calling earlier. I guess you were at a friend's or had the ringer turned off."

"Yes, Mother, that was it."

"Well, I wish you would turn the ringer back on at all times. You never know when I might need to get hold of you right away."

"Okay, Mother. Speak to you next week."

Back to the Future

Such was the unspoken life back in the Sixties. And, back when you were becoming who you are today, practically everything was about the future—aside from your family history, you were essentially traveling light. At sixty, however, you have real baggage…steamer trucks and U-Hauls and maybe even a boxcar or two of stuff from the last 40 years. And a lot of that stuff not only weighs you down and anchors you to the good earth, it has some legal holds on you.

So when you move in with someone over sixty, you're moving right into a lifetime of lives which are intricately connected to your new roommate or housemate. No new leaf. No wiping the slate clean. Just as when you have sex with one sexually active person, you are also potentially passing along sexually transmitted "material" from an exponential number of previous partners (and their partners)—sorry for the unfortunate image of an Heironymous Bosch mass orgy in which you are the one at the bottom of the pile—such is the reality of the late-in-life living arrangement. Sexual or platonic. True love or Friends with Benefits. And if you are having sex with your roomie, re-read Chapter 7.

Be aware.

Dr. Marj Steinfeld, a psychotherapist from Montain Lakes, New Jersey, who counsels clients on creating peace and love in their inner lives (including external living arrangements) and who once shared her home with a good friend—and the friend's teenage daughter—for over a year, knows the terrain well.

Dr. Steinfeld says that the most important thing to do before talking about moving in together is to get to know—really know—what your future roomie is like when no one is looking. She suggests simple things like going out to dinner together: "Is she or he nice to the wait staff, generous with a tip, patient when something goes wrong?" She adds that, if possible, it's also a good idea to go on vacation or a short road trip with your friend. There's nothing like sitting next to people for eight hours in a speeding cage to learn about their bathroom habits and what they need from their companions.

Before moving in together for good (i.e., selling out or giving up the old lease), she strongly advises instituting a trial cohabitation period where housemates learn each other's more intimate lifestyles, not to mention their idiosyncrasies. Are they neat freaks or slobs? Organizers or go-with-the-flow types? Glass half-full or half-empty? Lemons or lemon-ades? Risk takers or not? Socializers or not? Talkers or not? Confiders or not? Do they need music going all the time? Or the TV? How interesting are they? How interested are you? How interesting are you?

Marriage??? At Your Age??? Why???

Well, lots of reasons that you could figure out yourself. But don't go into marriage as a naïve sixty-something Pollyanna. Be extra mindful if, basking in your second hippiehood, you disregard common good sense and propriety and decide to tie the knot. Not so fast, Nellie.

Dr. Steinfeld says that a late-in-life marriage can be a wonderful thing, but it could also be a minefield of powerful disappointment. "If a couple is going to get married," she says, "one of the first things they should do is to get themselves a new place to live." Both partners need to feel at home, and unless you gut the old place, it's still going to be his house or her apartment. His bed. Her furniture. Her toaster. His rug. Her taste. His smell. Her photos are not only on the wall, but when you take them down, they leave a fade mark in their place. His ex-wife's or ex-lover's coffee cups.

Then she mentioned the dirty words, "Get a pre-nup."

Prenuptial Agreements

Despite the fact that prenups are now an integral part of the language of marriage (they're all over TV and movies—and the popular film "Intolerable Cruelty" was completely constructed around a lawyer who could create iron clad pre-nups), I suspect that most people don't really understand what a pre-nup is or what it is designed to do. And, while it does seem a romance killer for the twenty, thirty, forty, and perhaps even the fifty-year-old set, it is potentially an incredibly important aspect of senior luv.

So, what is a pre-nup? A prenuptial agreement is a private agreement between a prospective bride and groom in which they agree upon the disposition of their property in the event of death or divorce. It is designed to override or clarify the law, that otherwise would apply. Simple enough...or is it?

Arlene J. Dubin, the author of *Pre-nups for Lovers: A Romantic Guide to Prenuptial Agreements* and partner at Rubin-Baum LLP, where she specializes in matrimonial law, is a staunch proponent of prenuptial agreements. She asserts that upwards of 20 percent of all marriages today are preceded by prenups—and that by 2020 she expects that 50 percent will be effectively pre-nupted.

In her book on pre-nups Dubin outlined twenty-four reasons to engage in a pre-nup, but in a recent exclusive interview she identified the two primary reasons for such a legal agreement: "The number one reason (to establish a pre-nup) is that the divorce rate in our country is almost fifty percent. Another reason is that the divorce laws in our country are subjective, and judges have a great deal of discretion." She also mentions the facts that a) The median duration for a first marriage that ends in divorce is 6.3 years (which not a really long time) and b) 75 percent of people who divorce will eventually remarry (which is a lot of people). The combination of those two facts suggests that it is not only wise to consider a pre-nup, but even wiser to do it.

And One Reason to *Not* Do a Prenup

New Paltz attorney Andrew Kossover has a slightly different take on the question of whether to pre-nup or not. After handling hundreds of divorce cases, he has come to the conclusion that in his estimation there is one compelling reason to consider *not* having a pre-nup. "It really does take away from the romance, if only momentarily. You have to deal with that." I might add that real life—everyday life—tends to take away a little of the romance of romance. Yet, at a time when couples are swept up in that giddy emotional high in anticipation of living "happily ever after," having to think about money, divorce, death, and other decidedly undreamy subjects is like raining on the parade.

Kossover explained in an interview that if both parties are entering marriage on a "level playing field" (i.e., their net worth is about the same)—another compelling reason to have the "lay your cards on the table" financial discussion during your engagement—there is probably no compelling reason to write a pre-nup. Nevertheless, he counsels that all engaged couples "... be honest with each other. Take a minute out of the romance to talk about your financial status—and your expectations for sharing the wealth. Then you'll know whether or not a prenup is really necessary.

"You also have to check how your home states regard assets in divorce," he adds. For example, in New York exixts what is known as Equitable Distribution Jurisdiction; that is, husband and wife are considered economic partners in marriage—and in the case of divorce, money/support is awarded in context with how much time and sacrifice has gone into building the couple's assets. If husband and wife are married a long time and during the course of that marriage a certain amount of equity was built up, both partners are going to share as equitably as possible in the sale or ownership of that property. However, if most of the wealth was gained prior to the marriage—and the marriage itself did not last very long—then the distribution will be quite lopsided in favor of the wealthier partner.

In contrast, California considers all assets "community property" upon marriage—and thus each partner immediately shares an equal standing in his or her mate's financial holdings (or debt). It doesn't matter how long you are married or how much you contributed to the profit or loss—it's half yours.

The bottom line? Find out what the deal is in your state. You can't play the game effectively if you don't understand the rules.

And what do you find at the bottom of the bottom line? Beware of your own generation's lifelong inclination to not listen to good sense. Know thyself.

Chapter Ten

The Older People's Pharmacy

Hey! Mr. Tambourine Man, play a song for me.
—Bob Dylan

*S*everal years ago when I went down to Boca Raton to help move my aging parents closer to the family (i.e., closer to my now sainted sister Marj in Jersey—it's always the daughter, right?), I had to travel around to seven different pharmacies, large and small, mega mall and strip mall, to fill my father's prescriptions before we left town. No joke.

Annoying? Yup. Absurd? Of course. Dangerous? Absolutely.

Funny? A little, but only in retrospect.

Funny like when my old man, aka Mr. Moneydoesntgrowontrees, used to drive ten miles out of his way to save 2 cents a gallon on 29 cents a gallon gas ("Highway robbers, I tell you!"). Not so funny was the reality that in all likelihood none of my father's seven pharmacies and seventeen or twenty-seven or thirty-seven pharmacists knew what other drugs the man was taking—and neither he nor them knew of the potential drastic interactions for any of the multiple medications because no one knew everything that he was taking ("The whole lot of them …doctors, lawyers, mechanics, politicians, they're all highway robbers!").

Unfortunately, this is not simply an isolated case of an irascible old man trying to save himself a few shekels. Indeed, it's all too common that senior citizens shop around for deals on drugs. Before you sink back into that 442-horse power, Indian bedspread-covered Barca Lounger of smug satisfaction and take comfort in the illusion that the inventors of the Early-Bird Special were clueless in the extreme, please know that it's not just our parents' generation who played that self-deluding mind game. Former beatniks, hippies, yippies, and rapidly aging yuppies are apparently jumping into the old man's Oldsmobile and driving off to pick up scripts at three-four-five-six-seven different malls. As my old friend Bill Sheeley told me as we sat in the cluttered back room of his pharmacy, "It's not just multiple pharmacies, it's multiple doctors, sometimes prescribing the same drugs, different doses."

It's not just about penny pinching, though it is that too. It's also about hoarding, getting scripts from several docs and stockpiling supplies. For what, I don't know. Armegeddon? The next Depression? The icecaps to melt? The end of Social Security? LBJ, Richard Nixon, Janis and Jimi to return from the dead and have a beta-blocker party? Nuclear war with Native Americans (who have been waiting 200 years to get retribution)? Resale? I don't know.

Here it gets more surreal: From all available evidence, it is also about simple embarrassment. Hard to imagine that a generation that danced naked in the mud and rain at Yasgur's Farm and naively thought we coined the term Free Love, would grow up (well, grow older) to be bashful about our bodies. Yet it turns out that many of us don't want people we know to know what's up—or not going up—or just down with us. We are definitely not letting it all hang out. So we get our STD meds at Rite Aid in Yonkers, our Viagra at the CVS in White Plains, our anti-depressants at the Eckerds in Scarsdale, sleeping pills at the brand-new Stop and Shop in New Rochelle, laxatives and hemorrhoidal suppositories at the old Walgreens in Hartsdale, and, for those with late-in-life diagnoses of ADSD, our Ritalin from the Target (pronounced Tar-sjay) in Bronxville.

I wish it would be different, but it is what it is. "I am you and you are me and we are all together." Same shit. Different generation.

*

When I first conceived of this book, I planned on interviewing some hotshots I'd been referred to from University of Wisconsin School of Pharmacy and Albany School of Pharmacy—and maybe even catching a quote or two from Joe and Terry Graedon, who penned the uber-famous and, at the time(1976), uber-radical *People's Pharmacy*. But as I started the actual writing I began to understand what the real issues were all about and that as a dues-paid member of the Question Authority generation, I had an obligation to avoid the kind of canned answers that anyone can get off the Internet or the overloaded self-help shelves at Barnes and Noble. I realized that by interviewing "big names"—for this chapter or any others for that matter—I was not only taking the road more traveled, but I was driving my father's silver Coupe de Ville right into the deep, deep, deep ruts that forever separated his generation from ours. Which, for lack of a better set of words is simply a cop-out. Thus, this chapter—this book—is not so much a guide to self-evident information as a terrestrial guide to the outer limits of post–sixties consciousness. Hang on.

All things being equal, which they never are, by the way, the last thing any of us need is another book, another chapter, another resource offering us the same ol' same ol' expert info that you can get at the Sam's Club of information—i.e., the World Wide Web—which, judging by the extensive addictions to drugs and authority in this country, no one listens to. This book is about looking at the world ahead of us through a different set of eyes—the same eyes, though a bit more myopic and tired (though not quite so bloodshot) than they once were, that saw through the duplicities of the world and ultimately re-envisioned the culture of this country. Our eyes.

So I didn't contact the Graedons or Oprah or those post-doc pharmaceutical researchers who supposedly wrote the book on drug interactions. I went to people I could actually trust. People who know me and my pharmaceutical needs better than anyone on earth: my local drug dealers, Jack and Bill Sheeley, proprietors of the local non-Rite-Aid, non-CVS, non-Wal-Mart Dedrick's Pharmacy on Main Street in New Paltz.

Practically every time I walk into Dedrick's, I have a "Cheers" experience, only the chorus isn't "Noooorm!"; it's a nod, a smile, a comment about the weather or a question about the kids. It's Susan S., whose daughter went to school with Bay; it's Jeannie W., who knows Addie, Nancy, and Cael. It's Jack Sheeley who looks over the tall display of vitamins and calls me "Stevie"—Stevie!—sixty-one years old and he calls me Stevie, a name I haven't been called since I weighed 75 pounds and thought I was already much too old to be called Stevie.

Jack and his brother Bill have been dispensing life-saving and pain-saving drugs to me and my family for thirty-four years. I haven't actually been in this situation, but I know I could call up Jack or Bill in the middle of the night and get an emergency prescription filled. I know that one or the other of them would rouse himself out of bed, get in the cold car, and drive down to the pharmacy so that I or someone in my family wouldn't suffer.

Indeed, those two good men know more about my chemical history—and my family's most private medical information—than anyone alive. They have been with me and my generation in this town since we made the move from acid to antacid, from mushrooms to Metamucil, from alpha-states to beta-blockers.

A cautionary pharmaceutical tale: when *Time* magazine, in a tell-all story about Rudy Giuliani's ex-wife, his paramour, and his prostate cancer, mentioned saw palmetto as way to maintain prostate health, the saw palmetto industry went through the roof in profits. I subsequently asked a family practitioner if I should take it and he shrugged and said, "You're past forty, why not?" I then asked my urologist if that was a good idea. He said it was. And it was later confirmed by my internist—and reinforced by the wan and skinny gurus at the local health food store who sell a thirty-day supply of the stuff for $30—and later reinforced by the Balch and *Balch's Guide to Nutritional Health*, which advises 320 milligrams per day.

Slam dunk, right?

So I went to Bill and Jack to ask their opinion. They said flat out that saw palmetto is only marginally effective and the downside is that regular use can mask much bigger and more dangerous prostate problems.

So, after all the expert advice, I went with Bill and Jack. No saw palmetto. In fact, I don't fill any prescription by any doctor until I ask the brothers first.

Why? Because I trust them. Simple as that. You gotta trust somebody in this life and they're the ones I rely on for my drug info. They know medicine better than any doctor I've ever met because that's their job. I can't ask anything more of anyone whose product I put into my body.

So here's what they said about a few other highly important drug issues relevant to those of us from the Sixties for the sixties:

• **The good news: Medications have been improved by leaps and bounds over the past ten years.** This is especially true of diabetes, cardio-vascular disease, chemotherapy, blood pressure, and cholesterol control. The greatest changes are occurring on the hormonal level, and these are creating profound effects on related systems and organs. According to Jack, the new generation of drugs is not just extending lives, which they do, but they actually save lives. If you had a stroke in the 1990s, you were pretty much in the same predicament that you would have been in during the 1890s or 1790s—the ol' wait-and-see, which translated means you're either gonna die or lose use of one side of your body for the rest of your life. Today, it's not only possible to save your life but to counteract many, if not all, the harmful long-term effects of the stroke.

• **The cost of prescription drugs doesn't really vary between mega drug stores and local mom-and-pop storefronts.** You may save money buying your toothpaste at CVS, but Jack says that "Insurance companies drive the pricing for all pharmaceuticals," so anyone who has health insurance or is a Medicare recipient is simply not going to save money shopping around.

• **Most common conditions which require meds for the over-60 squad**: Diabetes ("Out of control" says Bill), cardio-vascular conditions, and "Metabolic Syndrome"—pre-diabetes, elevated blood pressure, high cholesterol, and high blood sugar. "These are people who have never had a heart attack, but during a physical exam it would look as if they did."

• **Medicare prescription drug program (Medicare Part D)**: The only real choices concern how much you want or need to pay into the system on a monthly basis (generally $0-$250). The monthly nut will reflect your co-pay.

• **The Medicare Part D "Donut Hole"**: Plans differ, but in general for the first $2000 in one year, you must fork out a twenty percent co-pay. For the next $2000 or so (Jack says typically four to six months), you pay a considerably larger portion of the costs (discount negotiated by Medicare)—this is the Donut Hole. Then it's a 5 percent co-pay for all prescriptions after that. So…you're okay for a while, then eating Kraft macaroni and cheese for several months (just like the old days), and then you're back on-line at the old early bird specials again.

• **Generics: Parts is parts, right?** It stands to reason that if the generic is made up of the same chemicals as the brand name, it should have the same effect(s) on the consumer. Right again? Not so. It turns out that there are significant differences in absorption rates found between brand and generic drugs. And absorption rates often determine how effective or ineffective a particular medicine will be for anyone taking that drug. Simple as that. Not so simple is the way in which the differences in absorption rates can be traced directly to binding and particle size and, just as important, the ways in which individuals process or metabolize any given drug. Thus, two individuals with similar medical profiles may have strikingly different responses to the same drug. Some of us do as well on generics as we do with brand names. Some don't. And some don't do well at all because the binding properties or the particle size (don't ask) prohibit effective utilization. So, nothing new here. The only way to find out if something works for you is to try it—and in the process, tend to your own garden.

• **Mail-order pharmacies**: Picture yourself at one of "those" parties in 1969—you walk in and there's a candy bowl full of different color pills (and, of course, other kinds of paraphernalia artistically placed on either side of the candy bowl). At first, it appears as if you're in for a wonderful ride somewhere in the cosmos this evening, but then a rare moment of clarity occurs to you: A Woodstock version of your mother is sitting on your shoulder squawking, "Get that out of your mouth! You don't know where it's been!" Only she's not talking about the half dollar you're pressing between your lips, or the practically uneaten Nutty Buddy you found on the floor of the Woolworth's. She's talking about mail-order and Canadian drugs.

According to my experts, Bill and Jack, both options are real crap shoots. In terms of Canadian drugs, you need to know that Canada is not just buying pharmaceuticals from America, they are purchasing goods from the world market. Thus, for better and worse, there is no FDA "watchdog" to oversee production and distribution. And as such, there is an increased probability of ending up with contaminated, inconsistent, and counterfeit drugs.

It only gets worse with Web or mail-order drugs: beyond the issues related to Canadian drugs, you simply do not know where the medicine has been between the sender and your mailbox. You don't know if the meds have been exposed to broiling heat or subarctic cold. You don't know if the drug has been switched, diluted or tampered with in any way. And then, of course, there's the problem of the stealing drug shipments from mailboxes.

*

My prescription for a good drug dealer in your old age? Go to your local pharmacy. Make friends with the pharmacists. They know drugs. They know you. They know your brain on drugs.

Chapter Eleven

Ganga For Gramps

"When I was in England, I experimented with marijuana a time or two, and I didn't like it. I didn't inhale, and never tried it again."
—Bill Clinton

While my kids were in high school, I would be asked periodically to come in and talk about the Sixties for a sociology class offered by a Mr. Rodriguez. Frankly, it was fun to be the resident hippie, though I found myself slightly hippier with each succeeding child as I sat on the edge of the teacher's desk. I would smirk that old Sixties smirk and, with very little encouragement, tell outrageous tales of protests and be-ins and happenings and free love and free speech and freedom itself, fielding endless questions from kids who have grown up to imagine the era to have been one big, fun-filled hallucination.

Each year during the presentation, some kid in the back, often with chronic bed-head would awaken from his school-induced stupor, glance hesitantly at the teacher, and then ask with a slightly raised lip if I ever smoked weed. The whole class would break out into laughter, of course, all eyes suddenly darting back and forth between my embarrassed daughter or son and Mr. Rodriguez, who would audibly inhale and hold his breath, wishing, hoping, and praying—per Dusty Springfield—that he would not lose his job. Then all eyes would turn to me.

(Here's a facsimile of the internal rhetorical monologue going on in my head: "Should I be honest and tell the truth—unlike most adults—and risk condoning bad behavior? Or, do I lie, thus committing another bad behavior and perpetuating an untrue myth about how well-behaved I and my generation were, despite our reputation for having consumed every street drug known to human kind? Do I stumble into the despised 'Don't trust anyone over-thirty" demographic?'")

And then, as if sensing some burgeoning inclination to revert to my hippie ways and let it all hang out, to get to the real nitty-gritty, as it were, Mr. Rodriguez would finally respond to his own oxygen deprivation and exhale, sputtering out something along the lines of "Let's use Mr. Lewis' precious time to discuss issues of greater social import than the drug culture."

I still don't know what greater social import he was talking about, but the conversation inevitably moved on to something "safer," like the Vietnam War and Free Love and the Dow Chemical demonstrations.

No one ever asked if I still light up. (I don't.) But that would have been the more interesting question.

*

>*"Baby Boomers' use of marijuana and other drugs is increasing, while drug use among teenagers is declining... The use of illicit drugs among Baby Boomers 50–59 rose 63 percent from 2002–2005, according to the survey, sponsored by the federal Substance Abuse and Mental Health Services Administration."*
>—Donna Leinwand, *USA Today*

Very interesting, indeed.

Although it's an unfortunate truth that as a generation we've been too often guilty of believing that we invented everything from sex to death, it's clear that getting high is older than Mel Brooks' 2,000-year-old man. As that wild and crazy guy Friedrich Nietzsche wrote in 1882 "Who will ever relate the whole history of narcotica? It is almost the history of 'culture,' of our so-called higher culture."

To wit, some rather interesting historical figures assumed or known to inhale:

- Louisa May Alcott, author of *Little Women*.
- John Hay, secretary of state under McKinley and Roosevelt.
- Bing Crosby, !#$%^&*?! I don't know what to make of this.
- Jack London, author of *Call of the Wild*, who once wrote

about a hash experience: "…Last night was like a thousand years. I was obsessed with indescribable sensations, alternative visions of excessive happiness and oppressive moods of extreme sorrow. I wandered for aeons through countless worlds, mingling with all types of humanity, from the most saintly persons down to the lowest type of abysmal brute."

• Margaret Mead—arguably the most famous anthropologist in the world. She testified before Congress in favor of the legalization of marijuana on October 27, 1969, and she told *Newsweek* in 1970 that she had tried it once herself.

• Robert Mitchum, who actually got cuffed with actress Lila Leeds in 1948 on charges of possession and got sentenced to 60 days at an honor farm. He later was quoted as saying, "It's just like Palm Springs without the riffraff."

• Diego Rivera—considered the greatest Mexican painter of the twentieth century. *The Book of Grass* contains an account by the actor Errol Flynn telling how Rivera asked him whether he had ever heard music come from a painting. Holding out a joint, he said, "After smoking this you will see a painting and you will hear it as well."

• William Shakespeare. Yes, Bill! Some South African researchers from the Transvaal Museum in Pretoria analyzed pipe fragments found on the grounds of his home in Stratford-on-Avon. The findings, published in the *South African Journal of Science*, show that eight of the pipes tested contain traces of cannabis and two of the pipes contain traces of cocaine. Others appear to be laced with tobacco, camphor, and hallucinogenic nutmeg extracts high in myristic acid.

• George Washington—only slightly more shocking than Bing !#$%^&?*!—Washington's diary reports that he separated males from females in his hemp garden, "rather too late." Much speculation has ensued about whether or not Washington's reason for sexing his plants was to make a more smokable product.

And, of course, long, long, long before the so-called civilized types were lighting up, indigenous peoples everywhere were known to have used cannabis, peyote, and other narcotics for religious and recreational uses. Closer to home, split equally between the functional uses of hemp for binding things and lighting up the stuff for various non-functional, unbinding functions of mind travel, marijuana cultivation began in the United States around 1600 with the those degenerate Jamestown settlers. During the nineteenth century, marijuana plantations flourished in Mississippi, Georgia, California, South Carolina, Nebraska, New York, and Kentucky. Between 1850 and 1937, marijuana was widely used throughout United States as a medicinal drug and could easily be purchased in pharmacies and general stores. Starting in the 1860s, the Ganja Wallah Hasheesh Candy Company made and marketed maple sugar hashish candy. In Philadelphia, during the American Centennial Exposition of 1876, at least one pharmacist sold hashish.

Okay, so human beings have been getting high since fire was invented—enough of the Wikopedia nonsense. Thus, it shouldn't be a shock that, despite all the profoundly silly and terribly wasteful time and money spent in our lifetimes on "The War on Drugs" and Nancy Reagan's "Just Say No" program and all those unbearably stupid and yet laughable "Here's your brain on drugs" ads, an enormous number of folks are still lighting up and, as a result, getting down.

Even folks who send other folks to prison for smoking pot.

I love this ironic report from the BBC News in Rome about Italian members of Parliament caught in a drug sting: "In secret tests for a number of illegal substances the programme said 16 of 50 lower house deputies tested positive for cocaine and cannabis. Almost a third appeared to have taken the drugs in the past 36 hours."

Even ultra-conservative William F. Buckley of the *National Review* is hip to the fact of marijuana as a fact of American life: "A Boston commentator observed years ago that it is easier for an 18-year-old to get marijuana in Cambridge than to get beer.... It requires less effort for the college student to find marijuana than for a sailor to find a brothel. Still, there is the danger of arrest (as 700,000 people a year will tell you).... The obverse of this is increased cynicism about the law.... Two of every five Americans, according to a 2003 Zogby poll, believe "the government should treat marijuana more or less the same way it treats alcohol: It should regulate it, control it, tax it, and make it illegal only for children."

I'll get off the soapbox now. The bottom line is that a lot of good, red-and-blue-stated Americans are still toking up; and in denying that reality, lawmakers are running around high on something much stronger and more dangerous than a doobie.

That reminds me of Philip Levine's poem "Gin," about teenage life in the Fifties, which ends with the line, "Any wonder we tried gin."

As famed chef Emeril Lagasse might say, let's kick it up a decade with a variation on the theme of "Gin":

Beyond
Our fifteenth birthdays, lay
The Bay of Pigs, the JFK assassination, the Gulf of Tonkin Resolution, the draft
LBJ, Agent Orange, MLK assassination, RFK assassination,
The Tet Offensive, Mai Lai, Kent State, and the political acumen
of Henry Kissinger, who brought us
Richard Nixon Redux, complete with wife and dog
And the Watergate break-in.
Any wonder we got high.

And then once more thirty-five years later:

Beyond
Our fiftieth birthdays, lay the lies:
Monica Lewinsky, the Supreme Court decision in Bush v. Gore,
WMDs, "Mission Accomplished" in Iraq,
"Brownie, you're doing a heck of a job" in New Orleans,
global warming, national debt, the Surge and the political acumen
of Dick Cheney, who brought us
Donald Rumsfeld Redux, complete with Wolfowitz, Halliburton,
Abu Grav, Guantamamo, and waterboarding.
Any wonder we're still getting high.

Thus, the question for this era is not why so many boomers are still turning on, tuning in and not dropping out, but that the whole country isn't high 24-7—or is it?

We're Not Just Getting Better, We're Getting Older

And sicker. And more susceptible to chronic everything.

Sorry, but at this stage of life, the ganga is no longer just a pleasant escape or a way to chill out after a long day at work or even to heighten the sensual experience of life itself, though it remains all that as well. For many present and former hipsters—virtually everyone I interviewed who also declined to be named in this book—marijuana serves the same purposes that the Manhattan or the Martini served for our parents' generation. But it is also, for many sixty- and seventy-year-olds, a way to maintain quality of life—it is a well-established option to circumvent pain and suffering, a way to extend life.

In fact, despite the decades' long "War on Drugs" and the unbearably stupid propaganda against marijuana use, a 2004 poll conducted for the American Association of Retired Persons (AARP) has found that nearly three out of four older Americans support legalizing the medicinal use of marijuana. Overall, 72 percent of respondents responded affirmatively that "adults should be allowed to legally use marijuana for medical purposes if a physician recommends it."

Lester Grinspoon, professor emeritus of psychiatry at Harvard Medical School reports in his book *Marijuana, the Forbidden Medicine* that cannabis is an excellent choice for reduction of symptoms related to:

- cancer chemotherapy
- osteoarthritis
- premenstrual syndrome
- bipolar or manic-depressive disorder
- pseudotumor cerebri
- diabetic gastroparesis
- normal aging

Grinspoon and James Bakalar, J.D., lecturer in law in the Department of Psychiatry at Harvard Medical School have developed a website, rxmarijuana.com, where you can find first person narratives about the efficacy of marijuana for all sorts of problems related to above list, as well as:

- anxiety
- depression
- violence/anger management
- post-surgical pain relief
- parapalegia
- meningitis

In fact, Grinspoon wrote in the *LA Times*, "Cannabis will one day be seen as a wonder drug, as was penicillin in the 1940s. Like penicillin, herbal marijuana is remarkably nontoxic, has a wide range of therapeutic applications, and would be quite inexpensive if it were legal."

It's possible he's smoking too much of the stuff. But stay tuned, please, even as you tune out again.

Chapter Twelve

The Legacies of Woodstock and Vietnam

I've Been Through The Desert on a Horse With No Name
—America

---

*F*ree speech, free love, civil rights, long hair, beards, afros, bell-bottoms, tie-dye, dashikis, peasant blouses, Indian bedspreads, Vietnam, Mai Lai, Dow Chemical, grass, mushrooms, peyote, sweat lodges, acid, psychodelics, psychedelic rock, blues, funk, the first jam bands, flowers in your hair, be-ins, hootenannies, the VW Bus, Abbie Hoffman, Allen Ginsberg, Ram Dass, Prince Siddhartha Gautama, the counterculture, the Establishment, the Diggers, Haight-Ashbury, Easy Rider, the peace symbol, incense, communes, Charles Manson, LBJ, Beatles, sex, drugs, and rock 'n' roll....it's all a big bad joke and, of course, it's no joke at all.

But surrounding the big head rush that is 1969, like a tie-dyed headband are two defining events—one a war and the other a massive rally for peace and love—two historic events that make everything else look like fodder for the scrapheap of hippie history. In retrospect, even the famous walk on the moon, while every bit a giant step for mankind, pales in memory comparison. Woodstock and the Vietnam War are the bookends of our generation. They still split us apart today almost irreparably and, in looking back, they bring us all together again in shared passions.

As it turned out, of course, I missed both signal events of our generation. In 1969, like so many of my counter culture (read: white, middle-class) college friends, I made a stridently principled and correct, if embarrassingly naïve, stand against a wholly unsupportable, immoral war, which was raging on some 7,000 miles west of the Wisconsin-Iowa border. I used my leverage as a privileged white American to opt out—and, frankly, would have fled to Canada if the leverage hadn't work.

I was also more than 1,000 miles from Yagur's Farm on August 15, 1969, in a small cottage on Lake Kegonsa in Stoughton, Wisconsin, rocking back and forth and wondering what the hell I was going to do with the 10-pound pooping machine in my arms. (Given the lack of sleep and the undefined PTSD I was suffering from having gone from spoiled immature hipster to a spoiled immature hipster dad in a matter of seconds, it's more than possible that I didn't even know about Woodstock until after the event became national news—and maybe even a few days after that.)

In fact, much to my youthful egotistical surprise, the earth-shattering news on July 17, 1969, was not my son's birth. At St. Mary's Hospital in Madison, Wisconsin, where I was the first father ever allowed in the delivery room, the good nurses smiled behind their green masks and the fatherly obstetrician patted Patti on the knee and then shook my shaking hand. But that was it. There were no heartfelt embraces. No tears. No champagne toasts. This was a birth, like any other birth at in the obstetrical ward at St. Mary's—and, judging by the way everyone scooted out of the delivery room, there was apparently bigger news going on outside.

Out in the corridors it was as still as outer space. I'm not sure what I expected when I puffed up my boyish chest and pushed my way out of the swinging doors, but there were certainly no bands. No fireworks. No reporters from *The Capitol Times.*

As I walked down the hall that afternoon, peeking into rooms, I saw patients and staff all plugged into the airborn Zeniths—and from there into the cosmos where Neil Armstrong was less than seventy-two hours away from walking on the moon.

Frankly, I had never been much excited by rockets and space travel. The appeal of Superman, Captain Video, and later Captain Kirk had passed me by like a far-off meteor whizzing above my head as I was looking down at my feet. I always saw life in more earthy—or earthly— terms: the Brooklyn Dodgers, Camp Deerwood, the bounce of a leather basketball, my pal Richard. Later, it was Muddy Waters, a green Morgan 4/4, William Carlos Williams, a pitcher of beer, the Vietnam War, Patti. Patti. And Patti.

Then there was Cael, purple-faced and mush-headed and wailing like a police siren after a grueling twelve-hour labor and delivery. He was a real beauty. I called everyone I ever knew across the country, but most of them were not home. Then I raced over to the Rathskellar in the Union and found a halo-haired boy named Art Ohlman and a few of his friends sitting around a metal table on the shoreline terrace of Lake Mendota. I told them of the miracle of Cael's birth. Art smiled broadly and said his best, "Far out!," and gave me a big bear hug, but then there was nothing to more say. He was as far from the experience of young fatherhood as I was from walking on the moon. Or, at sitting in the mud at Yasgur's Farm.

Two days later, on July 20, 1969, Patti and I watched wide-eyed from her hospital room as Neil Armstrong stepped off the landing module and spoke his immortal lines. Everyone cheered in the corridors. Patti cheered. Cael yowled. Even I felt stirred inside by the magnitude of the event, but I was eternally annoyed that the fireworks and bands and corks popping all over the country were for the crew of Apollo 11, not also for Patti and Cael.

A month later as some of my brothers and sisters were rolling in mud at Yasgur's farm—and others were up to their necks in rice paddies on the other side of the world—I was sitting with my infant son on the rickety pier of our cottage on Lake Kegonsa, sunnies flipping out of the water. I dipped my bare feet in the cool water, the moon rippling out beneath the pier, and wondered for the first time what a father feels when his boy is called up to fight in a war.

What follows are some good, heartfelt testimonials about what I missed, here and abroad. But they are not simply reminiscences; they are offered as a kind of testament to our collective past and an admonition about the wonders and the consequences of the idealism that defines that past. I'm reminded of Abbie Hoffman's quote after the commercial success of *Steal This Book*: "It's embarrassing, you try to overthrow the government and you wind up on a best-sellers list."

Judging by the world that we helped to create following in the wakes of Vietnam and Woodstock, as the elders of the human tribe, we desperately need to get back to the Garden, but we need to get back there on a wiser path.

Woodstock ★ August 15–18, 1969

Gary Allen: By the Time I Got to Woodstock

On the first of "four days of peace, love, and music," we packed ourselves into a Dodge Dart and drove from New Paltz to Bethel. OK, somewhere *near* Bethel—we got to within nine miles of the festival. After an immobile hour or two, my Dart-borne companions were ready to turn back.

Not about to miss this historical event, I climbed out, hoisted a sleeping bag onto my shoulder, and started walking past the endless line of stopped cars. After walking *forever* in the August heat—when I was perhaps half-way to the festival site—heaven smiled on this weary traveler. It began to rain—no mere sprinkle, but a hippie-soaking downpour.

Imagine the scene: Thousands upon thousands of wet, tired, hippies (many with wet, tired dogs) along a twenty-mile long parking lot. Somewhere in the middle of this fragrant jamboree, a tall, skinny guy, wearing white bellbottoms, a shiny magenta, rayon shirt (with puffy sleeves—good lord, what was I thinking?), somewhat stooped under the weight of a water-logged sleeping bag.

Did that pony-tailed guy give up? No freakin' way!

Not then, at least—the next morning was a different story. I had spent the night cuddling up against someone I should *never* have been with, in that very wet sleeping bag. Did I mention that it was lined with some cheesy, yellow-dyed flannel—and that, at the first sign of moisture, it released that yellow dye all over the enclosed hippies? Did I mention that the sleeping bag was, itself, half submerged in the re-hydrated fecal matter of generations of Max Yasgur's dairy cows?

Enough was enough. I shuffled back down that same highway, and—when I reached some traffic that was moving—hitched a ride to New Paltz.

The white bell-bottoms, stained by God-knows-what-all was living in the mud of peace, love, and music, were never white again. No amount of bleach was to have any effect on them. I had to dye them a nearly fluorescent shade of magenta.

What can I say? It was 1969, and it seemed like a good thing to do at the time.

Gary Allen is a food writer living in New York's Hudson Valley. Published widely, his most recent book is The Herbalist in the Kitchen.

Linda Drollinger: Hospitality

Every summer of my young life, the influx of tourists from New York City strained rural Sullivan County's resources, services, and the fabric of its inhabitants' daily lives. In August 1969, I was going on 17 and looking forward to my senior year of high school in September. Of course we locals had heard about the Woodstock Festival, mostly dire predictions from the town fathers about the mayhem it would cause. But no one I knew had been able to get tickets, and many of the artists scheduled to appear at the festival were unknown to my conservative, small town peers. All we knew for sure about the festival was that it was aimed at the counterculture, a world apart from ours. My father ordered my brother, my sister, and me to stay far away from the main road that ran the roughly four miles between our home and the festival site. In direct defiance of my father's orders, my 15-year-old brother hopped on his bicycle and rode to the site to see what it was all about. By the time he got there, the gates had been overrun, so he walked right in.

Meanwhile, back at the house, the festival had found us. Unable to drive on roads clogged by traffic more than 100 times greater than that for which they were designed, festival-goers left their cars and camped on the roadside. To my father's horror, his five-plus acre property had become an impromptu campsite. Emboldened by need, the campers asked for food, water, shelter, and restroom facilities. My father explained to them that our water came not from a municipal supply but from our own drilled well, and so was finite in amount and subject to contamination from their make-shift restroom activities. Finally, a woman begged for water so that she could breastfeed her newborn infant. My father relented. As fast as we could, my mother, grandmother, sister, and I made sandwiches by assembly line and drew milk cans and gallon jars full of water for the campers. We stopped only when we ran out of food and jugs. It was the first time I'd come up against the experience of displaced people. And I realized then that, in time of crisis, politics, ideology, and social norms go by the wayside and people meet each other heart to heart.

Linda Drollinger is employed as office manager for a project team at NBC Universal, and lives in Westchester County, New York. Her spare time is devoted to a long quest for an undergraduate degree and frolicking with dogs of indeterminate breed.

Larry Feldman: I Was There. And Everything Was Okay.

I had just graduated from high school and I took a bus from Port Authority in Manhattan to Bethel in upstate New York. The bus got snagged in traffic several miles from the site and let us all off to walk our way in. My friend Jay Seltzer and I immediately noticed a comely young woman wearing a very sheer blouse that left very little to the imagination. We nodded to each other and I said, "I guess we're here."

There were long-haired guys and hippie girls everywhere walking up the road to the festival. It was tribal and terribly exciting. My buddy and I actually *paid* for our 3-day tickets, which were never collected. Having bullshitted our parents into allowing to go, we thought that we were all set. We were traveling light: two sleeping bags, no tent, no change of clothes, other than underwear.

We entered Yasgur's farm and carved out a section of dirt, soon to be mud. Good cheer and hippie vibes surrounded us. Friday's music was mostly folk—Richie Havens, Arlo Guthrie, and the lovely Joan Baez, whose clear voice mesmerized us. Then it started raining like hell; our sleeping bags and clothing were soaked and we fell asleep that night with the announcer's admonition: "That guy next to you, man—he's your brother."

We were wet and cold but we were half-a-million strong. My parents were probably watching the news and understandably panic-stricken, but they would hear from me soon.

I don't think that I realized at the time that I was part of an historic event. Although I did not smoke pot, did not have sex that weekend—it was happening all around me. I was there. And everything was okay.

I still have the hippie brocade shirt that I wore to Woodstock. I cannot fit into it now but it serves as a talisman for that magical weekend. Jay Seltzer and I hitchhiked back to Yonkers. That was the last time I ever saw or heard from him. Hope he's okay.

Larry Feldman, age 56, is a lifelong resident of Yonkers, NY. Married for 28 years to Jill, they have two children, Jennifer, 25, and Matthew, 22. He and his brother own an engineering and manufacturing firm in Bronx, NY.

Irene Berner: How I Lost My Job

My boyfriend Barry and I decided to leave Brooklyn on Thursday night, which was a good thing because we were able to drive right in and park inside the gates. We did not have tickets, but that didn't seem to matter because we got in anyway. We had planned to meet up with our friend Marty, who had the tent we would be using. Without knowing much about the venue, the plan was to meet up somewhere on the grounds on Friday. By some miracle, we found him and had a tent to sleep in.

I can't remember exactly when and where we bought a watermelon, but we had one for the weekend, and were able to trade and get all sorts of things for a slice. I was shocked, as I stood at the foot of the stage on Friday afternoon, to see that Richie Havens had no upper teeth—I had no idea.

I had a clerical job in a bank that summer and, since I had just started and was not entitled to any time off, I decided to call in sick from the site. This was before cell phones, so I stood in line for quite a long time waiting to call the boss. And because I must have called either person-to-person or-station-to-station, the girl who answered the phone knew that I was not sick at home and ratted me out to the boss.

We left on Sunday, when the rain stopped. We stopped at the Red Apple on Route 17 for a hot meal, and I couldn't wait to get home and take a long hot shower.

The media made it seem like everyone there was naked, because they kept showing a clip of a few people skinny-dipping. Not me. But I was teased mercilessly on Monday about running around naked all weekend long. I still have a few pictures of that weekend.

Irene Berner and her boyfriend Barry got married the following summer, had their first child in 1972, and the second in 1977. They owned and drove a taxi in New York City for about ten years. Today Irene is a certified financial planner with her own company.

Beverly Wallace: My Childhood Lightning Bug Summers Lit up the Hillside

When the clarion call to Woodstock sounded, we awoke. There was no formal invitation, no media blitz. All we knew was that there was to be a concert in a field upstate and we would be there. Better than Fillmore Hall in San Francisco! Better than the Avalon! Better than the Fillmore East on New York's Second Avenue in the East Village! All the rockers of our time were to show up for a great event. Who could ask for anything more satisfying on a hot August weekend than meeting up with friends, good music, cheap wine, and weed?

The thing was, the massive traffic on this country road, mostly used by farmers and an occasional hunter, slowed to a halt. People chatted amiably among the Harleys, VW buses and bugs, convertibles, dusty claptraps, old Ford pickups, many with painted flowers and peace signs on their rusting chasses. Townspeople came out to wave and wonder at the motley band of pilgrims. They took off their round hats and stood in shirtsleeves and black vests, puzzled by the snaking traffic jam. These were not the Amish my schoolbooks had portrayed with black hats and thin beards. These were Hasidic Jews in family getaway summer camps.

We pulled into a lane where a farmer let us park in his dusty yard. We climbed across his pasture, down a tractor path, through a stand of cool trees and up the other side.

I had never seen so many people before. We were at the top of a rise; thousands sprawled down toward a stage with an immense light-and-sound scaffold. We had skipped the admissions gate by coming through the farmer's land, but no one had tickets, anyway. Who paid to hear music in the great outdoors, ever?

An ice cream truck, listing horizontally in a ditch, was mobbed as the driver abandoned hope and handed out his melting profits. People streamed by, seeking a spot of land on which to sit. Our blanket abutted our neighbors on all four sides. Our backs rested on the heels of three bikers who immediately bummed all my spare cigarettes. They gracefully shared their beer as the afternoon progressed to sunset and we became fast friends. A swaying mother in a long, cotton Indian skirt, holding a dirty-faced baby, sat directly below us and immediately ate our food.

The evening descended; the music began. Singers and bands tumbled one after the other onto the makeshift stage. Helicopters hovered in and out as new performers arrived. They played, we watched, and the weekend ran on our energy.

When the rains came, we ran for the cars, nothing to do but sleep in them, under them, anywhere there was dry turf. We were boxed in and couldn't leave. We were mud-soaked, with streaked, grimy hair and no change of clothes. Some washed in the cow pond, brown and unpleasant. Others gave in to the elements and swathed themselves in dirty shirts and smeared their faces like mud-pie contestants with no adult supervision. Our farmer let us use his outdoor shower and we slept in his damp barn.

It was black night, late, and the performer onstage quietly asked us to light our matches, lighters, and candles. All my childhood lightning bug summers lit up the hillside. The people were shooting stars shining in the darkness, as a song was sung around us, upon us, for us. The song ended; flickering lights expired. Silence and night returned. We had become the event. We were the Woodstock Nation.

> *Beverly Wallace is an actor, playwright, and painter. Her plays have been produced regionally and off-off-Broadway. She has acted in theatre in New York and in Melbourne. Her paintings have been shown on two continents. She is widowed and lives in Manhattan and Australia.*

Vietnam ★ 1961–1975

Then there was Vietnam…the other part of the sixties. The darker side. And no, I wasn't there either. Partly out of conviction. Partly out of immaturity and selfishness. Partly because I was born white and middle-class and had options poorer and darker boys did not have. While many of us were making love, not war—and let's be straight about this, I am *not* apologizing for protesting an illegal and immoral war or for believing so wholeheartedly in John Lennon's plea to "Give Peace a Chance"—but there were oh so many of us who are now around sixty who for the most honorable reasons imaginable fought in the war and others who were killed decades before they got to reflect back on a life well-lived over sixty years, that I can't in all good conscience just leave the Summers of

Love (1967 really, but there were caravans going to San Francisco in 1968 and 1969 as well) to reminiscences of Woodstock. We were in Vietnam, too. Hundreds of thousands of our generation were there. More than fifty thousand lost their precious lives. Untold numbers are still suffering and struggling with the effects of that conflict. There have been 100,000 suicides of Vietnam vets since the war officially came to a close.

*

Adam Holloman: A Memory of Jimi in Dong Ha, 1969

All Along the Watchtower, by Jimi Hendrix, was sent to me in Vietnam, by my brother, and was playing on some hill in the DMZ, north of Dong Ha, as we watched a Huey shot down by mortar fire, over a mile away—and we couldn't help. . . . More lost and gone stories. . . Loved Jimi.

> *I found this story at war-stories.com, but was unable to locate Adam Holloman. It is reprinted with the permission of the webmaster of the site, Don Poss.*

Owen Luck: My Long and Winding Road to Woodstock

It was Christmas and I was home on leave before shipping out for my first of two tours of duty as a medic in Vietnam. Music became the mile markers of this journey and "Sgt. Pepper's Lonely Hearts Club Band" would signify the end of my life as an innocent, even though I was already a soldier, because as it turns that out no one survives war. And it was the music that allowed us to get crazy enough to not go insane.

. . . So there I was about to march off to war to the beat of the Beatles, my copy of Dalton Trumble's *Johnny Got His Gun* in hand. Next stop: Travis Air Force Base, San Francisco. Bernard B. Fall's *Hell in a Very Small Place* aside, I would soon be on my way, ". . . leaving on a jet plane, don't know when I'll be back again."

With the Tet Offensive raging half a world away, I spent my last night in the U.S. roaming Haight-Ashbury in San Francisco, hanging out with another GI and two topless dancers we met playing topless pool. We made it to the Winter Garden, copped a squat on the floor with some

Hell's Angels who responded "patriotically" to my haircut. I kept think-ing about how Albert King, BB King, John Mayal, and the Blues Breakers jammed, how Janis Joplin raged, and how Jimi Hendrix lit his guitar strings on fire and played the flames, while at the other end of the world, men were jammed between a rock and a hard place fighting and dying in a bloody battle to reclaim tactical superiority over a desperate enemy ablaze with the flame of revolution.

In Vietnam music would continue to play an increasingly vital role in my surviving every day in a world where the staccato of automatic weapons punctuated the rumbling tympani of the high altitude arc-light bombing missions colliding with the earth composing a symphony of death. The Masters of War were about to bring new meaning to music appreciation to this kid from New Jersey. Once "in country," it was not very long before I found myself in an Evac. Hospital. There was this guy from Philly who would every morning blast The Rascals' "It's A Beauti-ful Morning." Though vastly superior to reveille, the dichotomy of the reality of two worlds hit me hard as the bloody mass casualty of war filled the hospital to overflowing with blood and ravaged youth.

Later when I was flying as a "Dust-off" medic, another medic, David Ewing, called Little Bird, introduced me to the band Cream one day while I was singing along to Donovan's "Season of the Witch." We were friends until he was shot down and killed while I was on my second tour.

Operation Santa Claus would get me home in time to surprise my family on Christmas Eve. Between my two tours of duty I found the Beatles' "White Album" for my mystical Christmas present. "Ob-la-di ob-la-da life goes on there…," but by then I knew that life does not go on, not really. That idea is an illusion. Dying goes on is what goes on. Getting that backwards is no mistake,;it is just the way we cope with that idea.

The "White Album" was the musical muse of American pop cul-ture but that was a blur and before I knew it I was sky'n up my way back in Vietnam, where all along the real watchtower we continued to keep communism from invading San Diego. "And the Wind Cried Mary…."

Then it was over. I was on an Air Force hospital flight over the Pacific and within a week of my discharge came Woodstock. This was a real wreck. I started out with a bunch of friends and within a few hours of not getting anywhere they bailed. I was walking, then I was riding with two chicks from I-don't-remember-where who had no better an idea of where we were going than I did, but we were all going there together. After they gave up, I hitched a ride with some hippies from Greenwich Village. They had some remarkable acid and I was tripping in the back of a nifty, red, 1959 Caddy convertible, wind in my face when I realized that you really can "Never Go Home" again. This really was a trip.

At Woodstock it was raining and I was sleeping in the mud. This was no big deal, after a year and a half of backpacking for democracy, majoring in jungle warfare at the University of Southeast Asia. Suddenly there was a screeching explosion, "like heavy metal crashing into the earth." *In coming*, I thought, crawling for my life, trying to get small, trying to bury myself in the mud. *Cover! I needed cover! In coming!* Finally I crawled into something big and soft and warm and it was caressing me. And it was there that I found myself with Jimmy Hendrix playing the Star Spangled Banner, I mean the fucking National Anthem, surrounded by the arms and bodacious breasts of a big old blonde hippy chick. Finally I was home, cradled in the bosom of democracy.

> *Owen Luck served two tours of duty in Vietnam as an operating room technician and a dust-off helicopter medic flying Med-Evac missions. As a photojournalist in the early 1970s Mr. Luck covered the American Indian Movement at Wounded Knee in 1973 and with the Menominee Warrior Society occupation of the Alexian Brother's Novitiate in Gresham, Wisconsin in 1975. Eventually he settled into a twenty-year career as a location manager in TV commercial production. Currently Mr. Luck divides his time between his home in the Hudson Valley and the Pacific Northwest photographing Native Americans and First Nation Canadians. This work is presently collected in the Yale University Collection of Western Americana.*

Mike Powell: An Excerpt from "The Only Coward I Knew"

We were flying a combat assault mission into an area called Bu Dop—the American name for it was FSB Jerry. My bird was designated

Yellow 3 in the initial assault flight. The flight had been advised that there were Indians all around the area with the main force concentrated to the northwest. I think we broke south, but at about eight hundred to nine hundred feet, we began taking automatic weapons fire. I could hear the pop and see the tracers of all the fire coming up. It was my first "hot" LZ after leaving the security of my training aircraft and the security of my door gunner trainer, SGT David Jackson. But what happened next I dream about and second-guess until this day.

In the process of taking fire, our aircraft (Yellow 3, the wing aircraft for Yellow 2) took two or three hits, and Yellow 2 took a tracer into the fuel cell. My A/C (Aircraft Commander), David Herbert, radioed to tell Y-2 that they had flame coming out from under their bird, at which time they went into "fire on aircraft" mode, cut power, and headed for the nearest LZ guided by Herbert... As I tried to clear my M-60, to no avail, I looked one more time, and the aircraft was completely engulfed in flame; it was coming across the tree line to the targeted forced-landing area when the tail boom broke off. As we followed them in, Herb swung the tail around and we settled down at what I suppose was a safe distance, and my CE, Ron Leffingwell, and myself un-assed our bird and headed for Y-2.

The co-pilot, Lt. William Rambo, had gotten over the console and was coming out of the burning aircraft through the loading bay. As I grabbed him, this burned flesh pealed off into my hand, but he seemed to feel no pain. Ron had gotten the A/C out, and somehow we managed to get them onto 37deuce (our bird's butt #) when I grabbed my M-16 and headed back toward the downed ship.

Ron yelled at me to get back onto the bird, but I couldn't hear him and finally read his hand signals and understood what he wanted me to do. I asked him if everybody was out, and he said yes. It was at that point that I looked up and followed the smoke trail back out of the forced LZ and pointed to Ron that I was going into the tree line. You could hear rounds going off, and I had no idea if it came from the wood line or just rounds cooking off from the fire in Y-2.

He shook his head, pointed back to the aircraft, and let me know by the look on his face that I was to re-ass our own. I can never remember being torn between two things so much in my life. Even now. But Dave

Jackson had driven home to me that my first commitment was to my aircraft and my crew.

But then he was the one out there in the bush who could possibly still be alive and I was just leaving him there. But if I didn't do my job on my own ship, I could be endangering my crew and the two pilots we had just rescued. Therefore I remounted, cleared my M-60, and sprayed the wood line with 7.62 rounds until we cleared the LZ....

As they say, hindsight is always twenty-twenty, and I started beating myself up about not going back into the bush for the crew members. Then, while flying back to Tay Ninh to get the bullet holes repaired so we could fly back up to the AO (Area of Operations), I got the shakes. Ron tried telling me there was nothing that either of us could have done and that I had made the right decision.

But nothing anyone could say, (even) if it had been my own mother, would have helped the feeling that I had just deserted my two buddies, my hooch mates.... I don't know if I slept that night. If I did, it was fitful, and I was waking constantly. I never thought it would end. And, at the same time, I dreaded the coming dawn. Not only did I not have the courage to go back to look for Dave or John in the LZ, but I couldn't even mount my own aircraft to finish the mission that day.

I finally started flying again in two or three days; I'm not sure how many. Ron and I were awarded Bronze Stars with V device; our two pilots the DFC.... I felt mine was undeserved or misdirected, and I almost decided to take punishment rather than be decorated. I think the ceremony was temporarily postponed due to looking for me. I'd gone to get a haircut on orders from my platoon sergeant, PSG Whaley. But I was quite despondent.

So the only real coward I ever met while I was in Vietnam, I have to look at in the mirror every morning.... I'm not quite sure if I'll ever get past this. And I'm not writing this for any replies saying I did or did not do the right thing. This is only for me to judge. But I do know that Charlie has heard from Bryan, Dave Jackson's son. If he (Bryan) should read this, I only hope he believes I did what I did because I was a FNG and a scared twenty-year-old, half-way around the world in a strange land. My only wish is that I could have done more. My only memory is that I didn't.

*Mike Powell, a braver man than he ever knew, committed sui-
cide a short time after he wrote this note. The webmaster for the website,
Deanna Shlee Hopkins, gave permission to reprint this excerpt.*

Larry Winters: Coming Home

We'd spent two days quarantined on base before we could leave. We
used those days to celebrate our survival.

I received orders to Norfolk Virginia Naval Air Station. Dave was
bound for San Diego Air Station. Nile was off to Cherry Point, North
Carolina, and Tice and Plemons were both going to Jacksonville,
Florida....We raised beers, slapped shoulders and said our good byes. We
celebrated each other for surviving Vietnam and the Marine Corps and
for now, that was enough.

The stewardesses on our flight to LA were round-eyed, American
women, something most of us hadn't seen for a year. I stepped off the
plane in Los Angeles and in the distance a small group was standing
behind a gate waving. Green sea bags were hoisted onto shoulders and
we moved towards shrieking voices. Girls jumped up and down, moms
cried, fathers stood straight. Once through the gates, some Marines were
tackled with hugs, rocked, kissed, and pulled into the shoulders where
tears flowed freely. Most of us walked on past.

At the military customs gate the corporal asked, "You bringing anything back you shouldn't have?"

"No."

He waved me through without even looking in my sea bag. I stepped
through a set of double doors and, for the first time in thirteen months, I
stood in the civilian world. I made my way to an information counter
and asked where I could buy a ticket for New York. I got a flight that left
within the hour.

As I walked towards my departure gate, three men with long hair
and tie-dyed tee shirts pointed their fingers at me.

"Hey, look, there's one of those baby killers." They followed me at a
safe distance. I could hear them and after a few minutes I turned and stepped
onto the seats of a bank of chairs. One guy with love beads and a scraggly
off center beard said, "He wants to kill us, so he can notch his M-16."

I swallowed hard, trying not to jump at them. These guys had no idea of what I was about. Suddenly I felt someone take hold of my elbow. I turned to see a man in a blue pilot's uniform, "At ease, Marine."

His tanned face was rutted with wrinkles.

"Those kids don't have the slightest idea what you've been through. As close as they've gotten to the war is TV. Leave'em alone, it's not worth it."

"Who are you?"

"Marine Corps, Korea, Chosen Reservoir."

A set of gold wings with TWA printed on them was pinned over his left breast pocket. He let go of my arm.

"You're a Vietnam vet, aren't you?"

"Yeah, what's it to you."

"I'd like to thank you, for what you have done for me and our country." He said, stepping back and saluting.

"Thanks," I said, returning his salute. Briskly he turned on his heel. The three hippies had disappeared.

I arrived at Kennedy Airport six hours later and took a shuttle to the Port Authority bus station where I bought a ticket home. On the New York State Thruway I looked out the window at the green apple orchards and felt my eyes drawn to tree line. The bus turned off the thruway and down Main Street. The town didn't look like it had changed much. I stepped off the bus at seven in the morning. A few people stood outside waiting for the bus to Kingston. No one knew I was coming home....

The summer air was full of smells I'd forgotten. The bus driver dropped my sea bag at my feet. I picked it up and headed into the bus station to use the restroom. I sat my sea bag on a bench, went to the counter, and ordered an egg cream....

The sweet milky liquid of my youth slid into my stomach. The door opened behind me and I turned, squinting at the silhouette of a large man, the morning sun behind him. "Is that you, Larry?"

"Ray Conklin, how are you doing?"

He slapped me on the back. "You just get home?"

Ray was my dad's best friend. He and his wife Peggy played pinochle with my folks almost every Friday night. Ray had been in the Army Air Force in WW II.

"I just got off the bus."

"Let me give you a ride home."

"Ray, I'm not going home."

"Oh, I thought that's where you were headed. Where do you want to go? I own the taxi company here and this trip's on me."

"I'm going to my girlfriend's house."

He smiled, "Of course, let's go."

"Thanks, Ray."

It only took five minutes from the bus station to Sandy's house. In that short time Ray asked if I wanted to make a few extra bucks driving taxi. I told him I'd think about it. When I got out of the car Ray said, "Welcome home, son. Peg and I are going over to see your folks tonight."

"Ray, I'll have probably seen them by then but just in case I haven't, please don't tell them you saw me. I want to surprise them."

"No problem."

When I stepped onto Sandy's porch it seemed like a dream that had taken twenty years to wake up from. I watched my knuckles rap the aluminum door. There were no lights on inside. I guessed everyone was still sleeping. I knocked again. Sandy's mother Marie came to the door. She had a housecoat wrapped around her and was squinting to see me.

"What do you want?"

"Marie, it's me. Larry." I took off my hat and watched recognition set in. She undid the lock, opened her arms, and took me in. I held onto her for a few moments and asked, "Is Sandy up?"

"She's still in bed."

"Can I surprise her?"

"No, you can't. Go sit in the kitchen and I'll wake her."

I went to the kitchen and sat looking at the familiar gray formica table I'd watched Sandy do her homework on. I heard Sandy's voice and put my hands on my knees to keep them from shaking. I expected her to come right down when I heard footsteps on the stairs, but it was Marie. "She's getting dressed. You want coffee?"

"No."

"You two have waited thirteen months, you can wait another few moments."

"Larry, come upstairs."

Bolting past Marie, I took the stairs three at a time and at the top I fell into Sandy's arms. We stood a long time squeezing our bodies together, trying to make them touch in every place possible. She wept into my shoulder. Without letting go of her I walked us backwards into her bedroom, and kicked the door shut with my foot.

Larry Winters entered the United States Marine Corps after high school and served in Vietnam 1969–1970. Twenty-five years later, by then a licensed mental health counselor at Four Winds Hospital in Katonah, NY, the veteran returned to Vietnam with other heath care professionals to study post-traumatic stress disorder (PTSD) in the Vietnamese people and to make peace with his past. Larry is a widely published poet, men's group leader, and group psychotherapist. This selection is from his book The Making and Un-making of a Marine.

Chapter Thirteen

The Stairway to Heaven

Everything dies, baby that's a fact
—The Boss
In memory of my friend Steve Vermilye

Just as Rod Stewart rasped, "The first cut is the deepest," and Dylan Thomas said far more eloquently, "After the first death, there is no other," everything changes on that dime with which you used to be able to make a phone call.

The First Death of Our Generation

If memory serves me correctly, and even if it doesn't, Mrs. Gaynor would have packed enough Mott's apple juice, roast beef and turkey sandwiches, pears and apples, Oreo cookies, and, of course, paper napkins, to sustain the entire senior class at Wheatley High School. But this was no senior trip. And there were just four of us going to the president's funeral.

So it had to have been Mr. Gaynor who gathered us around the oval pine table in the dining room to give directions, though it's clear in retrospect that Mr. Kotcher, Mr. Diamond, and my father would have loved to have unfolded their own Rand McNally Eastern USA roadmaps and showed us, inch by excruciating inch, the way: the Long Island Expressway to the potholed Brooklyn-Queens Expressway to the Verazzano Narrows across Staten Island and over the Goethels Bridge to the New Jersey Turnpike. And so on.

Except for an emergency stop at the Walt Whitman rest area where Jon, the handiest of this unmechanical suburban crew, jerry-rigged the dragging muffler with a coat hanger, we headed straight south, crossing the Delaware Memorial Bridge and following signs to Washington, DC. It was just after 4 A.M. as we rumbled down Pennsylvania Avenue in the unnatural light.

To this day I can recall the bloodless feel of the minutes and hours following Principal Wathey's early morning announcement over the crackling PA that left the whole school speechless, and a few teachers crying. And, this image is forever immutable: Sometime later, in the midst of a boring assembly, I can see my track coach, Mr. Lawson, his face framed by the window in the double door, gesturing to another teacher out of my line of sight, a thick index finger sliding across his bared red neck. Richard, Mr. and Mrs. Gaynor's dark-haired golden boy gone gray and bald, says confidently all these years later that it was Marshall Diamond's idea to go on the trip. In fact, he distinctly remembers the room in the Kotchers' Old Westbury ranch house where the audacious plan was concocted.

The dark, melancholy line under hazy streetlamps leading to the Rotunda was miles long. A kindly cop on horseback said we'd never make it in time. He suggested that we drive out to the cemetery, twisting around and pointing behind us.

Somehow—I don't know how—we found our way out to Arlington before dawn, shivering down into the dewy lawn, no more than ten feet from the spot where groundskeepers would soon come to blow away the leaves and place a carpet of fake grass around the dark rectangular hole. We were there before the Secret Service men in dark suits staked out their posts. Before the spit-and-polish soldier with scrambled eggs on his hat politely kicked us out of the low branches of trees. Before the crowds, mostly adults looking like they were going to a fall picnic, elbowed their way in front of us.

And I do remember almost everything that passed before my watery eyes that chilly morning. The cassons. Nehru. Charles DeGaulle and his hat high above the other faceless heads in the cold crowd; my young, ageless despair over the wonderful and terrible fate of dreams.

Yet all these years later, I remain mystified that our over-protective suburban parents had actually allowed us to leave our houses at all that evening. And at 11 P.M. no less! Four seventeen-year-old suburban boys with combined social IQs that would be too low to pass Mr. Doig's American history midterm, piling into my Earl Sheib'd Ford

Fairlane, nicknamed the Green Weenie, and heading out for a rendezvous with history.

Certainly each of us tried the old dodge about how all the other mothers had already said yes, "... even Mrs. Gaynor." But I can't imagine why it would have worked. It never had before. Nevertheless, my mother, who was a cum laude graduate of the "I Don't Care If The President of the United States Allows His Children to...." School of Parenting, must have been mightily impressed by something.

Or maybe she and the others just knew that this was something not to be missed. Something their sons should never forget.

And I have never forgotten.

Even so, from my current vantage point as the father of seven grown children and grandfather of ten, I have to admit that I wouldn't allow any of my teenagers to leave the house in the middle of the night and drive five hours for anyone's funeral. "Go tomorrow morning, if you must," I can almost hear myself saying.

But, of course, for us that would have been too late. For some things, like births, weddings, and funerals, you just have to be there on time or you'll miss everything.

On cold winter days these days, when "a certain slant of light" through the dark woods reminds me again that I am no longer seventeen years old, I sometimes find myself wondering if we ever properly thanked our parents for their uncharacteristic indulgence and their remarkable remarkable prescience. I don't think so. (Gratefulness has never been a hallmark of our generation.) And four decades after the fact, it's already too late to thank George Gaynor, Zeke and Helen Kotcher, or my father, Samuel Lewis.

I also think how turning sixty changes everything, doesn't it?

D-d-d-d-eath

So...you can stick your fingers in your ears, wobble your tongue against your upper teeth 180 times per minute while humming "Alice's Restaurant," and do the frug, the mashed potatoes, or the chicken dance (your choice) all at the same time and nothing's going to change. You can train for a marathon, do 1,000 daily crunches, make weekly pilgrimages to St. Augustine, do monthly high colonics, get annual physicals, eat your

Wheaties, blend your organic juices, move in with Dr. Andrew Weill, swallow a half ton of anti-oxidants and make an appointment to get your face lifted, neck tightened and belly lipo-suctioned, and nothing's going to change. You can even pray day and night, night and day, to God, G_d, Jesus, Allah, Abba, The Buddah, Muhammed, Yahweh, Elohim, Deus, Jah, Ngai, Niskam, Bhagavan, Vishnu, Krishna, Mwari, and George Burns, and nothing is going to change.

You are going to die. We're all going to die, brothers and sisters. The Boss said so. Better get your house into order.

That was the sobering message that rose to the top of my old mental Eight Ball as I approached and then survived my sixtieth birthday. Honestly, it wasn't a terrible thought or a devastating revelation (like realizing that Jerry Rubin was just a con man), nor one that I hadn't thought of before. But it certainly defined the day for me. And in the process it helped define the rest of my life, which, actuarially speaking, is a mere fraction of what I've already lived.

Sorry to be so blunt. But it is what it is.

A Little Sorbet to Cleanse the Pallet Between the Heavier Courses

My favorite death stories:

• Phoebe Snedeker, a woman I read about years ago, got the solemn "Get your papers in order" talk from her oncologist and decided to forego the fruitless operations, chemotherapy, bloating, anorexia, and hair loss. As she was not yet feeling desperately ill, she made that audacious decision to live the rest of her life rather than sit around warding off death and signed on for a trip to the Galapagos(?????) with some friends. She was not a birder, but it turned out to be a birding trip. She found that she not only had a passion for birds, but a good eye for them, logging more birds in her journal than most of her fellow birding passengers. It was a great way to bow out, she thought as she returned home expecting the cancer to strike her down any moment. Which it didn't. So she signed on for another trip—this time intentionally seeking a birding excursion. And the same thing happened—passions excited, face flushed as she raised her binocs to see and identify more and more birds than any of her other aficionados. And, of course, as you've already sussed out, she returned home, prepared to die, only to find herself feeling alive and well—certainly well enough to take another journey…and another…and another until eighteen years had passed and the old bird met her maker in a car accident.

• Attila the Hun: a truly legendary bad guy and pillager, known by name by millions—even billions—who have no idea of what he did to earn his notorious rep (his army conquered all of Asia by 450 AD—from Mongolia to the edge of the Russian Empire). In 453 AD, Attila married a young girl named Ildico. On his wedding night he really cut loose, gorging himself on food and drink. Sometime during the night he suffered a nosebleed, but was too drunk to notice. He drowned in his own blood and was found dead the next morning.

• Tycho Brahe: Who? I never heard of the guy before I started do my research. Turns out that he was a hotshot sixteenth century Danish astronomer whose research led to Sir Isaac Newton coming up with the theory of gravity. Brache lived at a time when it was considered an insult to leave a banquet table before the meal was over. Known to drink excessively, Brahe had a bladder condition—but failed to relieve himself before the banquet started. He made matters worse by drinking too much at dinner, and was too polite to ask to be excused. His bladder finally burst, killing him slowly and painfully over the next eleven days. Nice.

• Jerome Irving Rodale: Founding father of the organic food movement, creator of *Organic Farming and Gardening* magazine, and founder of Rodale Press, a major publishing corporation. Rodale died on the "Dick Cavett Show" while discussing the benefits of organic foods. Rodale, who bragged "I'm going to live to be 100 unless I'm run down by a sugar-crazed taxi driver," was only 72 when he appeared on the show. Partway through the interview, he dropped dead of a heart attack in his chair.

Intermission's Over

In discussions about dying and death with psychotherapist Marj

Steinfeld (remember Chapter 9), she cut through all the psycho-babble and medico-babble and legal babble and wishful thinking babble and new-age babble and went right to the heart of the matter: The most important thing for the post-sixty crowd is to be conscious of the human condition. That is, anyone who is sixty years old is living with a scarcity of resources ahead of her or him, including time, energy, health, and even, dare I say it?, mental acuity. Mind blower!

Thus, the imperative (the imperative!) is to live the rest of our days, as we probably should have lived our youth, with intentionality. With mindfulness. With powerful respect for all that we don't understand and don't control in the incomprehensible universe in which we live.

Of course, that message is not terribly different than the one we've been hearing from all the philosophical hipsters we've been reading and giving lip service to over the past four decades—Gurdjieff, the Buddha, Jesus, Nietzsche, etc.—but now that time is running short, it should be right at the top of the spiritual grocery list.

In much the same way that Ram Dass suggested that we "Be Here Now," Dr. Steinfeld, who is 68-years-old and knows from what she is speaking, both professionally and personally, included several imperatives for living contentedly with a true consciousness of the human condition (which I have translated into a variation on the Timothy Leary triad):

• **Turn On**: Do not zone out. Ratchet up your vision prescription. Turn up your hearing aid. Find your voice. Find something important to do. Eat good food. Live each moment as if it's your last (it could be). Don't live the rest of your life drunk, high, or numb trying to escape the inescapable. Fear is paralyzing. The specter of death provides an extraordinary opportunity to live your life bravely and passionately—and I would say with a certain je ne sais quois hipness. To leave behind those matters of importance that the Little Prince warned us against.

• **Tune In**: Be as alive and awake as possible in each moment as it occurs. Eternity is found nowhere but in the moment we are alive. Read the newspapers. Listen with an open mind to what your children are telling you. Hear what their children are singing. Log on to the Internet to find out what you need to know about pensions, social security, medicaid, catastrophic health insurance, life insurance, living wills, wills, etc. Be mindful.

• **Drop Out**: Leave behind anger, self-righteousness, and pride, and the whole "should system" of life. Don't waste time going through the motions. Don't waste energy or mindfulness on pointless points of self-aggrandizement. Don't fill your days, live them.

The Second Death: Me Old Pal SV

In the days leading up to the big six-oh, I found myself thinking a lot about the old days around this hippie town…and in particular when my good friend Steve Vermilye built our family's house out in Springtown. It's a big, wonderful, cream-colored house with a long front porch overlooking a stream in the middle of deep-green woods. It is the kind of home that has done everything a house can possibly do to welcome, abide, and shelter everyone I love.

Back then Steve was a house himself. Broad-shouldered, big-bellied, thick-bearded, probably the most straight-up hammer-in-your-belt guy I've ever known. Solid as a house. Strong as a house. Full of stories like a house. And in a funky town like this, where folk-singing, dope smoking carpenters were as common as carpenter ants, Patti and I wanted no one but Steve Vermilye to build our house.

When I heard the impossible news that my dear old friend had died on June 19, 2001, I felt my shoulders sag like the roof of an old barn finally giving in to the elements. I thought I would collapse right where I stood, so I just started walking, hands in pockets, head slung low, around and around the outside of this big house that my old friend had built, my mind swirling with the summer clouds, legs wobbling with each step into the soft, sinking earth.

I knew Steve back when our babies were babies and the world had far more possibilities than memories. Back when he could carry Jamie and Lydia on each arm as he strode into the blue Atlantic. I knew Steven when he smoked a pipe, sticking an impervious thumb right into the burning bowl to tamp down the tobacco. I knew him in the pre-cholesterol hysteria era when he started each day with a butter-soaked, artery-clogging fried egg on a hard roll, lathered with a pound of salt. I knew him when we were so young that good health was assumed. When we believed that we would live forever.

We were wrong.

Steve was the first of the old hipsters I loved on this earth to take the big plunge. I'm not being cavalier about what is arguably the most profound passage of life right after the long journey down the birth canal. (And just for the record, I'm not talking about the projective grief many people felt upon JFK or Jimi or Janis or Jerry or, for that matter, the Big Bopper or Richie Valens or Princess Di crashing and burning in such a public way. I'm talking about real grief, personal grief, grief-grief, the kind that comes when you can recall that person's hand on your shoulder or rough beard on your cheek or the unguarded smile that crossed his or her face when you entered the room.)

Dying Well (Not an Oxymoron)

So I return to me ol' pal, Steve V., who could be a poster senior citizen for how to die with grace and, I was going to say dignity, but dignity is so over-rated, so let's go with that seemingly insouciant Lord Buckley-type hipness, which is regularly overlooked as juvenile. It is not.

The fact of the matter is that Steve took to death in a lot of ways much better than he took to life.

Like so many long-haired college educated carpenters of our generation, Steve initially found relevance and meaning in working with wood. He worked hard—too hard—when we all should have been young and easy under the apple bough. Taking that tool belt and plumb line maybe a little too seriously, he went from carpenter to craftsman to contractor, home inspector, and real estate maven, single-mindedly working days and nights, nights and days, weeks and months, months and years through good times and bad, in sickness and in health, for richer and poorer, until his marriage fell apart.

Then he got a little crazy for a while. He bought a motorcycle. He kissed lots of women. And, because life has some redemptive qualities, he stumbled into love again. And then he turned around one day and his hand was shaking uncontrollably from the cancer growing in his brain.

Which was when he started to really live again. Maybe not just live again, but live for the first time.

For two years, through ugly operations and gut churning chemo and the unflinching love and support of his two children and the woman with whom he fell in love (yes, she stuck around for the whole thing) and some friends (not me, I am deeply sorry and ashamed to say) who ministered to his failing body, Steven laughed more, sailed more, went on more vacations, kissed the cheeks of more people he cared for and thought thoughtfully about the vagaries of life than in all fifty-some-odd years before. He was fully alive, dancing and singing on the head of the pin of life, welcoming, if not inviting the day when he would slip off that mortal coil.

That's how I want to do it.

Dying Well: The Funeral Happening

As a function of being pivotal era in American life, everything changed after the Sixties...for us and the country. And while so much good came out of that era, it can't be denied that the selfless, egoless, flowered quest for peace and love somehow led inexorably to those Me, and then, Me-First decades of the Eighties and Nineties. And then this hideous emblem of life in the new millennium about "modern dying" from the *New York Times*:

> *"At a time when Americans hire coaches to guide their careers and retirements, tutors for their children, personal shoppers...trainers...whisperers...wedding planners...it makes sense that some funerals are also starting to benefit from the personal touch...some families are beginning to think outside the box-provider, said Mark Duffey of Houston, who last year began what he calls the first nationwide funeral concierge. For $995 or a monthly subscription fee, his company...has helped several hundred families plan their final rights...."*
>
> —John Leland, "It's My Funeral and I'll Serve Ice Cream if I Want To"

Shoot me.

With that wild blue yonder just beyond the reach of my increasingly color-blinded vision, I can't imagine a more absurd, more insulting notion to the primacy of a hipster's life than to hire some corporate suit (and please beware the corporate killer in ponytail, ripped workshirt, and

Birks) to get out the clipboard, the Blueberry, the anorexic assistant from Mount Holyoke, and work up the costly and pretentious details for your or your beloved's final arrangements.

Whatever happened to that glorious notion of a Happening just happening? I know, it's quaint and retro and maybe even a little pathetic to be waxing on about Be-Ins and Happenings and, may God rip my tongue from my mouth, hootenannies (I'll restrain myself), but what about the beauty of spontaneity or just hanging loose, which seems particularly appropriate when one has been finally loosed from the constraints of mortal existence.

To misuse a phrase I first heard back in the day, you have to learn to leave the table when you're no longer being served. As the great—and not yet late—Lou Reed said, "… stick a fork in it, turn it over, it's done." Just arrange to gather some people together whom you love or like— maybe ask your drummer friend to bring a drum, or the bagpipe/guitar/ accordion player a bagpipe/guitar/accordion, maybe a poem or two, three or four stories, some warm food, some wine, and whatever else aids in your transcendence, and see what happens. How about something like "Our friend/father/son/uncle/husband Steve has died. For everyone who cared about him, let's gather at the beach in Rodanthe and say some things about him to celebrate/commemorate his life on this earth. Amen." And then go toss his remains in the drink.

- No fireworks.
- No holograms.
- No videos with cheesy sound tracks. In fact, no videos, no soundtracks.
- No steal-the-scene guest appearances by Bono.
- No fund-raising appeals for spina bifida.
- No wine tastings.
- No door prizes.
- No apps. No tapas. Nothing shaken. Nothing stirred.
- No after-death drinks with umbrellas.
- Just sobbing and laughing.

I'm thinking now of the last lines of the late Raymond Carver's great poem "Last Fragment":

And what did you want?
... to feel myself
beloved on the earth.

What else would any seasoned hipster desire?

Day Three: Grand Celestial Travel ... Riding the Marrakesh Express

Joe Cocker
Delta Lady
Some Things Goin' On
Let's Go Get Stoned
I Shall Be Released
With A Little Help From My Friends

Country Joe and the Fish
Barry's Caviar Dream
Not So Sweet Martha Lorraine
Rock And Soul Music
Thing Called Love
Love Machine
Fish Cheer/I-Feel-Like-I'm-Fixing-To-Die-Rag

Leslie West/Mountain
Blood Of The Sun
Stormy Monday
Theme From An Imaginary Western
Long Red
For Yasgur's Farm
You And Me
Waiting To Take You Away
Dreams Of Milk And Honey
Blind Man
Blue Suede Shoes
Southbound Train

Ten Years After
Good Morning, Little Schoolgirl
I Can't Keep From Crying Sometimes
I May Be Wrong, But I Won't Be Wrong
Always
I'm Going Home

The Band
Chest Fever
Don't Do It
Tears Of Rage
We Can Talk About It Now
Long Black Veil
Don't Ya Tell Henry
Ain't No More Cane on the Brazos
Wheels On Fire
Loving You Is Sweeter Than Ever
The Weight

Johnny Winter
Mean Town Blues

Blood, Sweat, and Tears
More And More
I Love You Baby More Than You Ever Know
Spinning Wheel
I Stand Accused
Something Coming On

Crosby, Stills, Nash, and Young
Suite Judy Blue Eyes
Blackbird
Helplessly Hoping
Guinnevere
Marrakesh Express
Mr Soul
Wonderin'
You Don't Have To Cry
Pre-Road Downs
Long Time Gone
Bluebird Revisited
Sea Of Madness
Wooden Ships
Find The Cost Of Freedom
49 Bye-Byes

Chapter Fourteen

Choosing a Handle With a Little Heft and Hip in It

Her name was Magil and she called herself Lil,
But everyone knew her as Nancy

"Trying to define yourself is like trying to bite your own teeth"
—Alan Watts

*S*econds after our oldest old son phoned with his outrageous news, Patti and I leaned into each other giggling like third graders. He had to have been kidding…I mean, look at us: we're still hipsters, contenders, true non-believers, beach dogs. We have two kids in the house! We stay up way too late! We still do the wild thing! Patti's hair goes down to her waist, for heaven's sake! And I've got a damn ponytail! We even have a VW bus! And if that's not enough, we live in the mountains a half hour from Woodstock! Not Woodlawn. Woodstock!

Grandma and Grandpa, my ass!

Yet, in the profoundly humbling silence that followed our childish hysterics—picture nine-year-old Elizabeth with a decidedly parental scowl on her beautiful and smooth face—it seemed pointless to hope that there was a tongue planted in Cael's cheeky announcement. So suddenly there was a new and rather dyspeptic New Age old age wrinkle on the classic Sixties identity crisis.

Merely hearing our 26-year-old son speak the words Grandma and Grandpa—and then snicker!—made it instantly clear that Patti and I would have to jump the geriatric gates and choose our own grandparental handles before we got strapped with something completely and totally uncool. Thinking ahead: what if our snickering son's pre-ironic bundle of lovable DNA gurgled out something awful? And not just awful, but something awful *and* permanently humiliating? (I've been to enough French restaurants to see some truly intelligent and elegant people snap their heads reflexively when some drooling toddler calls out some goofy name better assigned to a pet than to a silver-haired picture of poise and grace!)

As the first of our hippie friends to enter the venerable old hall of Parental Grandness, I wanted to select a title with a certain meaning and heft. Something decidedly manly and ageless. Something hip. Hell, I reasoned unreasonably, I'm no grandfather. I don't resemble all those grandpas—like my dad—down in Boca Raton. I'm a father, a beatnik, a teacher, a writer, a hipster on the loose ... what else would the little newt possibly call me? *Dad? Man? Professor? Writer Boy? Hem?* Not likely.

I briefly considered *Czar* (as in Zarathustra); then *Duke* (as in Snider); and then as a bow to the most royal Velvet Underground, *Lou.* But none of them really fit. The light came on, though, right in the middle of a depressing conversation with my new-age mechanic who yelled across the hissing engine of my terminal 1986 Honda Accord, "What do you wanna do with this junker, Chief?"

Chief?

Wow...I have to say that I immediately liked the sound of that one. And so it was *Chief.*

Patti opted for the simple and elegant *Her Majesty.* Despite the proletariat crush of seven kids around the dining room table, a shaggy retrohusband of questionable descent, a woodsy address 250 miles north of the Mason-Dixon Line, and a propensity for Patsy Cline (red beans and rice, quilts, and Diet Coke), Patricia is a true, blue-eyed daughter of the Garden District in New Orleans. Groomed at the Miss Edith Akins Little School and later refined at the Louise S. McGhee School on Prytannia Street, the former Patricia Charlee Henderson happens to be the real article. It should have been a no-brainer.

Unfortunately, *Her Majesty* was not met with that old knowing Sixties nod. You know what I mean, babe. While a few people chuckled politely at the notion of unplugged *moi* being called *Chief* (and then probably turned away muttering about old men who need to grow up), *everyone* we told was plainly affronted by Patti's essentially well-chosen appellation. Just as all narcissistic teenagers seem to maintain archetypal taboos against the appearance of being conceited, it seems that most idol-worshiping American adults would love nothing more than to rise up and behead some uppity middle-aged woman who would dare call herself *Her Majesty.*

In fact, nearly two months after her royal ascendancy to grandmotherhood, when Patti dressed up as a queen at the annual Halloween Eve parade down straggling New Paltz's Main Street, her good friend Donna got so mad at her that she tried to steal her scepter. It seems that despite a well-known adoration of English princesses and their high colonic lifestyles, we simply don't cotton to royalty—or grand anything—in this ever-youthful culture. Even as a joke.

But, of course, this particular late-in-life passage is not a joke, even as a joke. So I'm not joking when I say that soon after our self-styled christening, it soon become clear to Patti and me just how treacherous it was going to be to boogie through this change of seasons with any grace—or, if you will, cool. In fact, in the middle of Yoga-lite class a few nights after Cael's life-altering call, I closed my eyes and visualized a blue swimming pool rather than a river. A few movements later (while doing The Dog) I actually envisioned Patti—the one who still scratches my itch—stepping up onto the deck of that glistening blue pool shamelessly wearing gold lame slippers and a sequined T-shirt that says *Let Me Tell You About My Grandchildren.* I knew then and there (deep-cleansing breath) that it would take the tenacity of a Cal Ripken to stop myself from donning lime-green Florida camo-wear and screwing a "Happiness is Being a Grandfather" license plate holder onto the rear end of my VW van, which would be suddenly transformed into a 1993 gold Mercury Marquis.

As the ever ebullient T. S. Eliot told us ("I grow old...I grow old.../ I shall wear the bottoms of my trousers rolled"), time marches ever forward, despite our self-defeating wish to keep it static. And despite the sometimes painful vision of the Rolling Stones' bony Mick Jagger still jumping around on stages worldwide, we are not exactly the same brand of hippies we once were. When you're old enough to be a grandparent, it's time to grow up (a little anyway), whether or not you're a grandparent. It's time to be who you are—no more masks, no more image-making, no more adolescent ego driving you to ruin.

And the first thing to do is to identify yourself by choosing a good, serviceable name. Find a name that is warm and loving—but also cool and wise.

One caveat before I go on: In your heart of hearts, you may still think you're 19 and headed out to a summer of love in Haight-Ashbury, but the truth is that you've moved on since then and the name you choose should not only reflect where you came from…but where you are today…and where you're going in the vast unforeseeable future. As Don Henley warned us so succinctly and so well, "A Deadhead sticker on a Cadillac" just makes you just look silly. So, whether it's a traditional name (one with resonance and heft) or one that marks you as a new-age grandparent (someone who knows the way by looking at the stars or crystals or the I Ching), pick a title that makes you—and your grandkids—smile. Pick a name that reflects who you are in your cosmic heart and soul. And, whatever you do, in trying to be unique, don't throw out the senior citizen with the Jacuzzi water.

The Eternal Grandma and Grandpa

Of course I can't choose a name for you—like your choice of wine or cars or living room carpet or antacid, it's got to fit you and your own needs. The traditional Grandma and Grandpa—and their seemingly endless variations—are simply beautiful, time-tested names that place the wearer in a cosmic relationship within the cycle of life. And in keeping in mind the mantra of *Be Yourself,* they are precisely who we are once we are there.

Even though I'm saying it, it basically goes without saying that there are hordes of nominal grandmas and grandpas everywhere you go in this country—literally thousands of thousands of us out driving the highways, standing at bus stops, on street corners, sitting in folding chairs at youth soccer games, rushing into early-bird specials at the Olive Garden and Red Lobster. And although many millions of us share the very same name, every one of us—every single one of us—is utterly unique to the grandchildren who adore us like they adore no other people in the universe. Just as remarkable, the name itself never gets worn out or old. While trendy names tend to run their course in a mini-generation or two, no one ever grows tired of the ever meaningful, ever resonant "Grandma" and "Grandpa."

Invoking a Legacy

That said, there are many grandparents and grandparents-to-be who want to put their individual stamp ("I gotta be me!") on the old moniker. There are those who wish to move themselves off the genealogical highways to drive the backroads with a less generic, more family-specific handle. For them, the legacy route is a wonderful way to step into the shoes of grandparents they have adored their whole lives and, in doing so, keep their memory alive.

After being shunned by friends and foes alike for her choice of *Her Majesty,* Patti chose Damma, the name she called her own beloved grandmother from Biloxi, Mississippi. Similarly, our good friend Bruce Schenker, wanted his grandchildren to call him Zede, the name he called his Brooklyn grandfather. In keeping one's cultural roots alive, Stacey, Bruce's wife, chose the traditional Yiddish, Bubby. And, Johnny Domitrovits, who immigrated to the United States forty years ago when he was 18-years old, wants Rory and Connor to call him the traditional name for grandfathers in Austria, Opa.

Jim and Sonja Hillestad, who live in Clearwater, Florida, but maintain a strong Norwegian family identity, wrote and told me that "Hans' boys call us Farfar and Farmor, which is Norwegian for father's father and father's mother. That is the old traditional way of referring to grandparents in Norway. That is also what our kids called their grandparents, Mormor and Morfar, as mother's mother and mother's father." However, Sonja adds a cautionary warning that we might do well to take into account as we choose our grand names: "… You should know, though, that Christian, Becky's 18-year-old, calls Jim 'Old Fart.'"

The Transitional or "I'm Not Old Enough to be a Grandparent" Name

Then there are what I call the popular transitional names—ones that are neither parent nor grandparent, but both. Popular examples are Papa, Mama Doris, PopPop, etc. Transitional names allow the bearers the illusion that they're actually too young to be grandparents—or at least young grandparents, whatever that really means.

The choice of these head-twister names may have as much to do with the age at which we make the great ascendancy from parent to grandparent. My father-in-law, Charles Crawford Henderson, who is a lifelong angler and who was in his late forties when granddaughter Annie was born, chose the name Pawpaw. This served dual purposes: It preserved his sense of being a youthful grandfather and reflected his lifelong passion for fishing (a pawpaw is a fish). Now, there are ten grandchildren and six great grandchildren calling him Pawpaw.

Like Charles, when my sister's children were born, my mother was in her early fifties—and by her own account she didn't feel "quite old enough to be someone's grandmother"—they called her Mama Lily (and my father, Papa Sam). They still do. However, by the time my first child was born a decade later, she had obviously grown more comfortable with her age and position in the cosmos. So my seven kids and my brothers' two call her Grandma.

Whatever the reasons for the transitional name, though, I think we're seeing more and more of these kinds of appellations as the Baby Boomer generation resists or actively denies the aging process. My sister, Marj, a psychotherapist from Montville, New Jersey, is called Mom-Mom by her seven grandkids. Good friend Tom Nolan answers to the name Pops. Another friend, Frank Ciliberto, Gramma Ciliberto's husband, is known as Poppa. And Ellen Hall of Laguna, CA, whose grandsons call her "Mom" (probably, she says, because they hear their Mommy Corina call her Mom), is beyond delighted with the illusion that any pre-schooler would call her Mom.

The bottom line is to call yourself whatever floats your particular boat. Just keep in mind that whatever you're called, you're not the parent (see Chapter 9). Just as you're always your kids' mom or dad, you're always their kids' grandmother or grandfather.

New Age Names

Okay, so the traditional or even transitional garb and its various accessories don't fit as comfortably as your old work shirt. Well, then you might consider the endless possibilities of being called something slightly more off the beaten track…something perhaps more fitting to your time and tastes. For better and worse, we are, after all, the generation that broke practically all the social rules. Just think back on all the social conventions that have passed into obscurity since the late Sixties.

So, if you're into Native-American culture, you could try on something like Crazy Horse or Pocahontas. How much fun would it be to ride up on the ol' BMW steed and hear little voices chirping "It's Sacajawea!" Or, if over the course of your own transition from SDS socialist to captain of industry, you might want to try on something like Boss or CEO. Here are some others:

- Smooth and Lyrical: Ol' Blue Eyes or Billie
- Animal Nature: Elk or Kodiak
- Beatnik: Cat or Chick
- Hippie: Jimi or Janis
- Seventies: Dude or Sweet Thang; Stud or Foxy Lady
- Military: Admiral or Sergeant Major

How royal and urbane would it feel to referred to as Granpere and Granmere or the Archduke and the Dutchess, or M'Lord and M'Lady? Or…switch gears and think of how memorable it might be to borrow a marketing tool from NASCAR: Try your favorite number—or the number on your high school basketball uniform. Number One, Three … Four…Five…all the way up to Ten, they all sound good. Never bigger than a hundred, though—it gets too unwieldy. And, of course, never ever, ever use Two. Certain things in this culture are archetypal in nature, including poop jokes, and you'll never live down the first time your five-year-old grandchild says to a neighborhood friend, "Let's go over Number Two's house!"

Journalist Jeremiah Horrigan, whose granddaughter is right at the edge of language, told me that he "…would like 'Big Daddy,' but will settle for anything other than Gramps."

I like Jeremiah's attitude, but my advice is to be a little more assertive in the choice of your post-Hippie-New Age name. Although a lot of people think it's cute to be laid-back and wait for the name to arrive via the toddler Sphinx, that plan of inaction could easily turn into a long-bad trip. As I mentioned above, you may get stuck with a name tag that promises only scorn and derision. Passive living is always a real crapshoot.

For some, like my good friend Bruce Schenker, the roll of the dice went well: He was just as happy when Ruby opted for "Brucie" rather than Zede. And, as it turned out, Tom Nolan's other grandkids call him Tom. But you'll have to trust me, there are countless others (not to be identified here) who are not thrilled with their grand monikers. Some of them are sporting buffoonish names into their dotage—and then into eternity—because everyone thought some utterly idiotic utterance sounded *kinda cute* at the moment.

And others, it must be acknowledged, are actually victims of pure vindictiveness by their children. That's when your beloved kids' faces light up with that preternatural glee of someone who's waited a lifetime for vindication at being called Puddin' or Pumpkin or Pisher or Petie or any number of the other "ie's" that follow innocent kids into their teenage years. It is then that they exact the full revenge they've waited their whole lives to heap retaliation on you. "Yes," they smirk after the two-year old garbles grandpa into a momentary laugher that sticks to you like one of those old "Kick Me" signs that bullies stuck to the back of your shirt: "That's perfect! Let's call him Ol' Gasbag!"

So choose a name—and choose it well—and wear it as if you're the hippest grandparent in Peoria. In fact, wear it like you'd wear a headband at the next Be-In or Hootenanny, whenever one of those odd cultural phenomena comes around again. Whatever name you choose, though, take some abiding comfort and solace in the fact that your grandchildren already think you're the hippest grandparent in Peoria. They will always and forever adore you no matter what you're called. As Gertrude Stein might have said: "A grandma is a grandma is a grandma."

Although it is indeed as difficult to define yourself as it is to bite your own teeth, the sound of a little voice calling your name is ineffably sweet.

Chapter Fifteen

Grand Alchemy

What a long strange trip it's been
—Robert Hunter

*W*ay back in what now seems the long, long-past twentieth century, 1997 to be exact, our sweet nine-year-old daughter Elizabeth Bayou-Grace could only be described as gangly, giggly, gabby, and altogether glowing with the glory of life. Only a goon would confuse her with somebody's aunt.

My dear, departed Aunt Betty Levy of Hollis, Queens, was an aunt: big as a house, warm as a home, and, to this eternal little boy, as old as the borough of Peter Stuyvesant's Manhattan. Betty Levy had a bosom that filled a room several moments before she squeezed through the doorway in that ubiquitous floral print housedress. She was a cheek pincher. A yeller. A kveller. A gefilte fish peddler. She also had a staggering pair of rosy-colored salamis that would sway beneath her elbows whenever she opened her arms to embrace her skinny nephew in a warm, bosomy, suffocating hug. After each breathless embrace she would always lead me by the yanked cheek into a steamy kitchen for some gooey dish that predictably tasted a whole lot better than it looked. "Here, eat this, Stevie. It'll make good doodies!"

That's an aunt. Not a 53-pound imp with pigtails and a flippy-floppy walk who would never—if it's finally true that DNA runs in families—have what traditionally constitutes a bosom. Breasts, yes. A bust, perhaps. But never a bosom.

Yet—of course you know where this is going—when the first grandchild graced this big family, little Elizabeth, the child of our uncontrollable middle-age spread, transcended her fourth grade skin and bones and metamorphosed into someone's aunt. Just as amazing, Cael, the infant of our radically thin youth, and his wife Melissa suddenly transformed themselves into becoming parents, just like Patti and me. Only we instantly became grandparents. Just like—but nothing at all like, you know—my parents, who became, voila!, great-grandparents.

So it goes.

The metaphysics of life's changes when viewed from the vantage point of sixty years are simply amazing to one who has always believed in an immutable core of self. One day you're the baby in a big unwieldy family, and then like a warm breeze across a beaded forehead, you're instantly transfigured into an Aunt Betty. Or, at least an Aunt Elizabeth. Or, most amazing to this nineteen-year old trapped in a grown man's aging body, a Grandfather. (I, too, was the baby in the family. My sister Marj practically wept, "My baby brother is a grandfather!")

The very moment that Clay Steven Lewis was alchemized from foetus to baby with a cosmic (or was it comic?) yowl, the geophysics of our remarkably small universe changed forever. A baby's first breath in the Piedmont of North Carolina that would shake and bend giant grandparent oaks in the mountains of New York.

Like a Penn and Teller magic act, in a split second there appeared one more chair at the long pine table; one more name on the answering machine message; one more imperative to wake up, do laundry, go to work, mow the lawn, nurse the sick, doctor the despairing, minister the needy, and pray and pray and pray for safe passage.

Believing that I was long past standing outside nursery doors, heart throbbing, listening for danger, I felt again the unmistakable burden of groundless love and skyless fear that surrounds new life in a family. The responsibilities of a life informed by babies are beyond listing, sometimes even beyond bearing.

Yet, as I welcomed my first grandson's profound weight on my arms and in my heart, the earth seemed to shift on it axis. Rather than feeling grounded—or at least anchored as one would assume all that inter-generational weight would do—I felt more buoyant than ever before in my fifty-plus years. Despite the anxiety about being a grandfather and all that that entails in my "Never trust anyone over thirty" mind, Clay's birth was not heavy at all. Not a burden. In defiance of the laws of gravity so clearly writ on a heartless bathroom scale, I actually felt lighter than I did in 1969 when Clay Steven's father lovingly grounded my free spirit.

Just like that…Abracadabra!…I was freer than I ever thought was possible in 1969. For the first time in nearly three decades of standing breathlessly at one nursery door after another—or sitting on the living room couch in the dark waiting for the sound of a car door slamming—I could feel my body relax and, if just for a teasing moment, the yoke of existence magically lifted from my shoulders.

If one's most basic purpose on earth is biological—that is, to keep the species alive and well—then Patti and I had with that first yowl fulfilled our destinies. After siring seven kids—the easy and fun part—and then fathering them through the pangs and arrows of everyone's outrageous fortune—the hard and sometimes rewarding part—I'm more convinced than ever that a child is a gift to oneself.

A grandchild, however, is an ungiven gift to that world, a cherub that lifts its wings and flies like a dove out of one's worn and weathered hat. A grandchild is nothing more and nothing less than a public confirmation of the most private affirmation of the goodness inherent in life.

So with that first yowl—and the knowledge that there would be a chorus of yowls to follow, adding to the concert—I suddenly realized that I didn't need to do another thing on earth to show my worth.

As my Uncle Murray (Aunt Betty's dutiful hubby) might have said, "I done it."

I knew in that transformational moment that, if little else, Poof!…I didn't *have* to write another word, though I still wanted to—and we certainly needed the cash. And Hocus Pocus!…I didn't *have* to teach anymore, though I still enjoyed the drama—and, with two kids still to raise, we desperately needed the benefits. And Presto!…I didn't have to prove anything to anybody. I could stop running the Look-At-Me-Look-At-Me! Marathon. I was officially off the hook. I'd done my job. I'd crossed the finish line (and done it without even knowing it was coming)!

And, standing there with a checkered flag in her hand, like a New Age vision of my Aunt Betty, was the formerly gangly, giggly, gabby, and altogether glowing with the glory of life, Aunt E. Right there in the smotheringly warm kitchen of my altered perceptions, I saw Elizabeth kvelling and yelling and applauding her tiny nephew, his brand spanking new parents and his born-again grandparents, those bony ribs puffing up up and away to resemble a full-fledged bosom.

I sometimes have to pinch myself (in lieu of Aunt Betty taking care of that job) to make sure that it really happened.

Let Freedom Ring

It happened. So it goes.

As of this writing, it's about to happen for the tenth time (Clover) with, again, the promise of even more to come. Miracle upon miracle, each one a phoenix rising out of the ashes of the daily Sisyphusian toil on this angst-ridden planet. As Yogi might have said with the benefit of a toke or two, "When it's over it's not over." As some old fool always says with real gravity in his voice every June at some high school graduation—as if it's never been said before—in some ways the end is just beginning. (And consider this: nine-year-old Elizabeth is now 18, a college freshman with a pierced eyebrow, a tattoo, and dreds.)

Transformation and change, flux and flow, movin' and groovin'...the veritable hallmarks of the 1960s. Change is life. The status quo is death. "The first one now will later be last." Having been altered at the molecular level in the cosmic moment of that first generational birth, I have found myself returning again and again with renewed eyes to Ralph Waldo Emerson's notion of consistency as "the hobgoblin of little minds" and Walt Whitman's yawping—"Do I contradict myself? Very well, I contradict myself. I am large, I contain multitudes."

I do—you do—contain wildly dissimilar multitudes.

And the first thing I think about from this lofty 60-year-high perch is to know—to admit—to summon up the courage to know that Janis (who was a mere 27-years old when she died) was wrong: Freedom is not "just another word for nothing left to lose." And so Kris Kristofferson (who wrote those startling words when he was in his early thirties) was simply too young and too arrogant to understand freedom.

Freedom is found in the substrata of the notion that there is a right and a wrong for any given situation...what psychotherapist Karen Horney called the "should system." Freedom is (suddenly!) being old enough not to care about all the stupid things that you worried about as a teenager trapped in an adult body. Freedom is being set loose from all the rules and regulations of parental life. Freedom is, in effect, being a grandparent happily saddled with three generations of contradictory needs and concerns.

Life itself has an interesting way of letting us know that many things that were so important yesterday are so insignificant tomorrow. First, you were someone else's kid and subject to all their rules of the house. Then, you were someone else's parent and making laws about living under your roof. And now you're free of all that. In effect, you're no longer responsible for all those always tedious and sometimes demoralizing life lessons. In this new world order, all the rules have changed.

And, all the rules have stayed the same.

And, if you get that, you get this from Aunt Stevie (Nicks):

The winds of change
Gonna blow it all away

Chapter Sixteen

With a Little Help from My Friends (and Family)

"Drivin' down the road, tryin' to loosen my load …."
—The Eagles

*I*n the midst of all the rubble that was left smoldering after September 11, 2001, came the soul-stirring announcement that our daughter Addie was pregnant.

The good news first sent me reeling backwards onto the floral couch, moved to clownishness (hands gripping my chest, ala Redd Foxx) by the suddenly ridiculous fact that our little girl, who once carried her dolls around by their hair, had grown up enough to be someone's mother. But soon thereafter it all—and I mean it all, from the fire and billowing smoke to the insidious threat of anthrax—sank in. So in the days after September 12th, I found myself slumping deeper and deeper into the soft cushions of the couch, my lower lip beginning to tremble, as fathers have always been brought to trembling at the ancient inability to protect our children from what H.L. Mencken called the Unknowable, "… calmly licking its chops."

As our ever-savvy television and radio execs extracted profit from the mesmerizing shockwaves of soul-shattering images transmitted into our living rooms all day, every day, I learned that even joy can be damn frightening. It was enough to make anyone not want to get up off the soft couch—or get out of bed. Certainly enough to make me want to turn my back on the leveled, jagged world outside this pastoral river valley and try to convince myself that refuge can be found here in the deep, green hollows in the Shawangunk Mountains behind our home, or by leaning on the rough-cut rail of the Facklers' horse farm, or in the smell of leaves burning in the fire ring next to the stream called Snowsoup, or in the cluttered aisles of the Ariel Booksellers off Main Street, or in a mouthful of my wife's warm and comforting red beans and rice, or her mouth on mine.

Or anywhere—just to find a place in my home and heart that was finally safe from the terror that invaded our lives. A sanctuary. Something impregnable to potect my pregnant daughter Addie, who stood in front of me, full of life, defying my fear.

Like every other prospective parent who has ever walked upon this imperfect earth, neither Addie nor her husband Jon knew what would lie ahead in the vast dark and unforeseeable future. Yet they somehow moved ahead with their lives, I imagine, bolstered by the irrepressible dreams and moonlit visions that have moved lovers since the dawn of time. They became for me the daily incarnations of Eve and Adam, valiantly setting forth from their own shattered gardens without benefit of map or compass or crystal ball. (They and the millions of others in every corner of the cornerless globe bursting with their own seeds of immortality.)

I'm not just talking about the ordinary life-altering changes a newborn creates in one's sleeping, eating, and sex habits. Bitten by the snake like everyone else in America, Addie and Jon suddenly found themselves walking away from the fearsome rubble right into the maw of uncertainty, calmly licking its chops.

As the father of seven whose children were born in a seemingly less frightening era, I can only imagine how daunting it must be to carry new life into a war. Even in more "normal" times, there are those oddly annoying strangers who seem to appear out of nowhere on grocery lines or in elevators with a warning, a superstition, a quasi-scientific fact, a rumor, a secret—all designed to scare the life out of you. But in the powerful wake of 9-11, when there was so much talk of gas masks and skin salves and antibiotics and poisoned water supplies, I found that Uncertainty itself sleeps with you, drives to work with you, sits down at the table with you at the end of the day, picks up a knife and fork.

Just before Halloween in 2001—just a month and a half after the Twin Towers collapsed in a heap of horror—Addie joined her mother and me on a long hike up the carriage trails along the Shawangunk ridge.

Her bright face was aglow like the leaves, her blue eyes as serene as pristine Lake Awostng at the top of our long climb. She was undaunted.

I don't want to suggest that there is any sense of redemption for the horror of September 11th in my daughter's stride, no balancing of good and evil contained within her womb. As far as I can tell, there is nothing redemptive about evil. But in looking back on that climb today, I am today awed at life's unimpeded persistence. I am stunned by the unwavering insistence of blood and bone and breath, at the arrogant courage of love that supersedes everything, including uncertainty and death. In Addie's glorious presence, I understood that life is more powerful, more enduring, more eternal than death itself.

The Beatles were right: "Love is all you need." And the Eagles too—"Take it easy."

After that day on the mountain, I borrowed some courage from my little girl. I turned off the television. Fred Friendly was never more right about the wasteland that it is. I got up from the couch. In the midst of the din of war I heard my wife, my life, calling. The family was around the table. I still had good works to do, mourning to share, blood to give, comfort to offer, doors to open. Bay and Elizabeth still needed me to drive them to soccer practice and flute lessons and the movies and eventually off to college. There were other daughters to escort down the aisle. Grandchildren who need a hand to walk them across the street, a chest upon which to lay their weary heads. I have untold unborn grandchildren who yearn to be adored by their grandfather.

I found that the most powerful force of all beckoned. As always, life beckons. And if there's a message or lesson in all that, it's just to keep moving ahead. We're genetically wired to do it. It's the only way out of whatever mess we're in. And as poets, philosophers, and watchmakers have been telling us for generations, time marches forward. Life beckons. The blood pulses.

Blood Simple

And there was Nancy, my baby girl, the infant of my unkempt youth (not that I've done such a bang-up job of kempting myself over the past several decades—check out the photo on my website), stopping in to say hello and casually dropping something of an improvised explosive device of a sonogram on my cluttered desk.

The conversation went something like this in real time:

"You're pregnant!" I exclaim, getting up to hug her with all my might and quickly plopping back down to catch my breath.

A demure if enigmatic smile flits across her face as I gaze at the swirling vision of my baby girl's uterus, replete with all the cosmic complexity of that startling phrase. "Looks like two peanuts," I say flippantly.

"Yeah." The enigmatic smile turns kind of smirky.

"Yup, peanuts, two of them," pointing my own smirky way at the curled tadpoles under the churning arc.

"Yeah?" Eyebrows raised.

"Yeah...Oh...Ooooh!"

A wide-eyed nod. A smile.

"Oh my God, there are two of them!"

The smile has now turned into a frozen grin as I imagine she ponders whether her father is as big an idiot as he seems. "Yup," finally, "that's what it looks like—two of them!"

The vision of identical twin boys on my desk was a powerful reminder of the magic that goes on in the universe right in front of our unbelieving eyes: like a Harry Houdini sleight of hand, the egg splits and *voila!* two babies where there was one.

Talk about virtual unreality. I closed my eyes and in a nanosecond I was transported to 3379 North Newhall Street in Milwaukee, Nancy's newborn weight in my bare arms, that small face turning into the soft white t-shirt over my chest. In what I thought was that long-lost spring of 1973 I'd lean on the smooth rail and peer into those dark marbles of eyes fixed on mine. I'd coo, warble, snicker, snort, snivel, and make some rather undignified high-pitched repetitive bird-like peeps, hoping beyond even unreasonable reason to make soulful and intelligent contact with that redemptive bundle of wonder on the fitted bunny sheet. But the toothless darkness behind the tiny circle of mouth would not answer. An enigmatic twitch here. A gaseous smile there. A mysterious arm flung up and dropped.

When Nancy got married, the joke around the family was that she'd walk down the aisle standing on my feet like we used to do while dancing to Willie Nelson's "Someone to Watch Over Me." Or riding piggyback. My baby girl. But, of course, bringing new life into the world is no joke. And bringing in twins was enough to turn off the laugh machine.

How would she get any sleep?

How would she take two babies to the supermarket?

How would she give two of them a bath? My Lord, how will she *nurse* them?????

*

And then there's this a few years later: I'm driving up Main Street in New Paltz muttering and blubbering and whining to myself about writing deadlines and piles of student papers and calls that need to be returned and emails that need answering and being in three places at the same time and what am I going to do about my ninety-two-year-old mother on Thanksgiving day…and how I sometimes feel myself slip-sliding away, sinking into an old kind of malaise, similar to that Vietnam despair but now it's Iraq and nothing seems to have changed in forty years, but even so it's way beyond that—it's about the unholy effects of religious extremism; it's about intolerance here, there and everywhere across the globe; it's about an overwhelming sense that the country is going straight to hell in a Hummer driven by a men drunk with power, skidding along a highway paved with anything but good intentions.

Which was when Clover reached out her lovely hand all the way from Boston and grabbed my wrist before I plowed into the guardrail and plummeted into Thelma and Louise Canyon. She called to say she's pregnant.

Our little flower who Tom Petty might have been thinking about when he wrote, "She's a good girl, loves her mama…loves horses and her boyfriend, too…." Another reminder that it's the audacious will of couples in love who, in defiance of a corrupt and indecent world, make beautiful babies and keep the lamps burning longer than physics and psychology would ever allow us to understand.

Life beckons. Always. From Conrad: "The meaning of an episode was not inside like a kernel but outside, enveloping the tale which brought it out only as a glow brings out a haze."

So I sit here in a kind of purple haze, glowing with life and the kind of grace that leaves me in awe of what we are capable of when we stop fighting the movement of the river. We got it backwards back then. It's not peace and love, it's love and peace.

Chapter Seventeen

Karmic Indulgences

Instant Karma's gonna get you
—John Lennon

$o there I was, feeling pretty much like the most depressing Leonard Cohen song ever composed (FYI, "Sisters of Mercy"), battered by property taxes and income taxes, a Mets losing streak, rising gas prices and cold, cruel, miserable rainy April days, not to mention the sights and sounds of all the lying, deceitful, dishonest, two-faced, double-dealing ("You Cheated, You Lied") testimonies before the September 11 Commission about what we're supposedly doing about terrorism ... and man, oh, man, I was headed straight into Ricky Nelson's "Lonely Town" when the beat finally picked up:

My wonderful daughter-in-law Melissa ("Sweet Melissa") went into labor, followed in due course by the cosmically magical appearance of one utterly gorgeous Madeline Elizabeth Lewis, eight pounds on the dot. Forgive the Laura Nyro reconstruction: one more high chair at the long table. One more chance to inhale that otherworldly baby scent. One more reason to hum along with Shades of Blue's 1964 summertime hit, "So in Love."

I mean, thank the stars for babies. They make your heart sing.

And, as these things go, you know, I affirm that my troubled heart sang that day and the dark clouds parted and the sun shone, the round world once again spinning perfectly on its axis as my daughter Addie and the little Princess Isabella arrived from Milford, Connecticut, to the tune of "Feelin' Groovy."

If you ever had the pleasure of meeting Adelyn before she was a wife, mother, and now a doctor of chiropractic, you might already have a good feel for what it was like to parent the beautiful little blue-eyed girl we once referred to as "The Bulldozer." The one primarily responsible for the orthodontically expensive gap in her sister Clover's smile from age five through ten. The one who, upon being scolded by me for being "contentious," immediately squared all 5 foot 3 of herself to full attention, looked me in the eye and spoke in military cadence, "Contentious: C-o-n-t-e-n-t-i-o-u-s, irksomely quarrelsome. Contentious."

If not, the following story might be instructive.

It is 1987 and I am picking up Addie and her friend Tiffany Ackert from one Andy Brown's birthday party. They're in seventh grade. If you need a period song, think "Mony Mony" by Billy Idol. I pull out of the driveway and ask rather innocently if they had a good time.

From right behind my head, I hear that familiar smirky voice: "Oh, yeah," followed by what I had already begun to recognize as a well choreographed pause-for-effect, "it was great; we all played spin the bottle."

From the far corner of the back seat I hear hand-over-mouth Tiffany giggles while I grab on to the steering wheel (to avoid being thrown from the fishtailing car) and go into instant parental crisis intervention inside my sizzling dad-brain: "Whoa, big guy, you were once in seventh grade, Addie's not the first of your kids to go to seventh grade parties, spin the bottle, this is no big deal, get a grip…remember the gas is on the right, brake is on the left, now, don't forget to stop at the stop sign, take a deep breath, make a left on Main Street and say, 'That's nice.'"

"That's nice," I say in monotone like one of the zombies from Talking Heads.

"Yeah," she says a little dreamily, "and I tried French kissing…"

Well, judging by the squeals coming from Tiffany's place in the back seat, I figure we're five or six seconds away from someone about to lose control of her bladder. And judging by the fact that all these years later, Addie and Tiffany are parents themselves, it's pretty clear that the lump in my throat didn't lead to the death of all three of us in a fiery crash.

However, I do remember Addie's perfectly timed punchline: "… but I didn't like it."

And that was just seventh gSrade. Life was often like that—and more—with the beautiful, vivacious, outrageous, c-o-n-t-e-n-t-i-o-u-s Adelyn, who is now—let the heavens rain down (think "Pennies from Heaven")—beautifully grown up and facing eternal retribution in the form of the beautiful, vivacious, outrageous, contentious Isabella, four glorious years old, going on a snappy twenty-four.

That's karma for you. Addie gave birth to the one baby who, by a unique combination of DNA and perfect cosmic design, would drive her mother to distraction. Utter distraction, that is. And some two decades after what I have come to call the Frenching Connection, I am doing the glorious karmic dance of 'what goes around, comes around' ("Turn, Turn, Turn"). I'm even tempted to do my Gene Kelly routine around a Main Street light pole.

Indeed, the joy of watching this unbearably cute, smart, sassy, loveable child do to her mother what her mother did to us all those years ago might be more spiritually heartening than all the church choirs in the universe belting out the chorus to "I Want to Know What Love Is." Or Old Blue Eyes walking down the sidewalk and crooning "I've got the world on a string, sittin' on a rainbow…."

And the best part of that is that she didn't really believe me.

*

Six months months later, the dining room looks like a scene out of Martha Stewart's worst nightmare: white curtains rustling in front of open windows, turkey platter and floral bowls on the sideboard, the long pine table crowded with coffee cups, half-full goblets of wine, paper cups with soda, small plates with crusts of cherry pie, a big spill on the tablecloth in front of Elizabeth, Addie's plump pugilist Jack Lewis squeezed into Bay's old high chair. Leaning back with a belly full of good food, I am for a suspended moment utterly amazed at what two clueless college students created simply by stumbling into love with each other in 1968.

When I turn my attention back to the buzz around the table, they are all laughing, swapping stories about growing up here in upstate New York. Addie is smirking as she tells about the time she jumped out of the hayloft on a dare from big brother Cael. "I was five," she says as proudly as if she's now no more than six. And everyone roars, except

Patti and me, who glance wide-eyed at each other in a kind of post-post-traumatic panic. *When you were five? That's gotta be twelve feet! Why didn't we hear about it?*

Then Clover, the mother of Schuyler, pitches in about how they all used to do *seat diving* in the school bus. "Seat diving!" I scream, but no one hears. She even gets up and demonstrates how they would stand on one seat and dive headfirst into the one in front while the bus was moving. I bellow over the giggling, "Why the hell did the bus driver allow you to do that?!"

They look at me like I'm a dinosaur. "There's a lot you don't know, Dad," says Cael, father of three, with a smarmy grin.

And as if to prove it, one after another of our grown kids, who we once thought we knew as well as the back of our hands, reveals some family history that makes me wonder if I'm sitting around a table with aliens who abducted my real children. There's the tale about turning little Jamie V into a human slinky on our steps, a couple of twitch-inducing stories about playing "doctor," one about Cael sneaking out of the house when he was grounded, another about what Danny and his friend Keith did the New Year's Eve they were seven. *Seven!* They howl at the phony phone calls, the nasty tricks they played on the sitters, the nastier tricks they played on each other.

And each time something new and awful is revealed, Patti or I scream "No!" in utter disbelief (and a desperate wish that if we say it fervently enough, it will be erased from the record).

The low point in this particular family history comes from Nancy, mother of the twins and karmicly beautiful Charlee (after the twins, she earned a placid child). Using carefully chosen phrases for the benefit of the grandchildren in the room who are sitting frozen in their seats hoping no one notices them, Nancy tells how she and Cael "walked in" on Patti and me one Saturday morning when she was four: "You were doing ... you know," her eyebrows arch—

"You walked in on us?" I gasped.

"Yup ...." Her eyebrows now look rather devilish.

Patti, barely able to speak, manages to squeak out, "I do remember once ...."

"More than once, Mom."

"But you never said anything!" my wife's voice rising like a whistle.

I scan the entire table. Five of them are nodding. The two with manners are studying the congealing turkey fat on their plates.

Patti and I have always prided ourselves in being very engaged—very in-touch—very aware parents. When the voice on the TV asks the eternal question, we *always* know where our kids are at 10 o'clock. But after the massive extended family rises like a posse and deserts us at the mess of a table, Patti and I just slump in plump deflatedness, wondering how so much could have gone on under this roof without us having a clue.

A few hours later, standing alone in the dimly lit hall, staring at a wall of photographs of smiling little urchins and their smiling, clueless protectors, I try to remind myself how much my parents didn't know about me when I was little. How much my mother *still* doesn't know about her sixty-year-old son. How history is always being written—and revised.

And with that bit of wisdom, I walked into the living room and told Addie as she fell back into the couch, completely and utterly exhausted after finally getting the Princess to sleep (three books, two songs, one promise of ice cream the next day), "Just you wait," pausing 1-2-3 seconds, "that little girl is going to turn your blue eyes brown."

And don't you know, it felt damn good; contentiously good.

Chapter Eighteen

Spare that Rod,
Spoil that Grandchild

Teach your children well
—Crosby, Stills, Nash and Young

Back in famous 1969 the Generation Gap seemed wider and more perilous than six rows of tracks at Grand Central Station. Today that once unleapable chasm is now crossed as easily as stepping onto a subway.

In fact, the space between the platform and the train has become so narrowed that when our first grandchild was born in Chapel Hill, North Carolina, there was no question that my wife Patti would be right there in the delivery room with our son and daughter-in-law. Put into time-warp context, my mother was a thousand miles away when our first child squeaked out his first breath.

In the midst of a cultural revolution of unprecedented dimension, our befuddled parents simply did not know who we were—and more often than not, where we were. In contrast, whatever clumsy missteps and bizarre parenting styles we "anti-establishment" types spawned over the past forty years, the defining fact of the Baby Boomers' parenting identity has been that we have not been strangers to our kids. For better and worse, we have been their friends besides being their guardians.

And although it's clear that we too often failed to act our age in the quest for familiarity, we learned more about pregnancy, birth, nursing, early childhood development, and adolescence than could ever be gleaned in one copy of Dr. Spock. We *felt the pain* of the "terrible twos." We *empathized* with our teenagers when previous generations of parents threw up their hands in confusion and disgust. We sent our teary-eyed children off to college as if they were going to camp, and when they graduated, we welcomed them back into their old rooms as if they had never left.

As such, our grown children have remained joined at our hips longer than any hippie might have once thought possible. Even as they got married. Even as they became parents themselves. Busy parents. Working parents. Professional parents. Parents who are now looking our way not only for babysitting services but for the same encouragement, support, solace, and direction they came to expect when they were children themselves.

It has left us in a unique relationship to our children—who are still are children—and our grandchildren, who are not our children. As it always is for this generation, up is down, down is up, except when it isn't, at which times up is not necessarily up, although down could be decidedly down. (Which, BTW, is terribly reminiscent of former Secretary of Defense Donald Rumsfeld's now infamous notion about what we know: "Reports that say that something hasn't happened are always interesting to me, because as we know, there are known knowns; there are things we know we know. We also know there are known unknowns; that is to say, we know there are some things we do not know. But there are also unknown unknowns—the ones we don't know we don't know."

If he wasn't talking about a miserable war and human beings dying in vain, then he would have leaped into the pantheon of my all-time hipster philosopher gods.

*

So…the question is…as our parents parents, do we act like parents to our grandchildren or do we act like our grandparents acted with us. Like Hemingway's Jake Barnes (in spirit at least, the equipment still works), I find that I mistrust people whose stories hang together. The world is simply too messy a place—and behind those hedges clipped at right angles and beneath those neat hospital corners are critters and snakes of every kind.

At sixty, I find the world to be weirder and often less predictable than I did back in my loopier days as a hipster, where nihilism paraded around a glass-half-full philosophy. From my limited view, the law of opposites seems most useful: Not only do opposites attract (people's evidence #1, my wife and me), but inherent in everything positive that we do, the opposite is present.

A wonderful example of the principle of opposites is found in TS Eliot's "Murder in the Cathedral": The doomed Archbishop of Canterbury comes to the Catch 22 realization that anyone who aspires to be a saint can never be saintly enough to achieve sainthood. Contained within the wish to be a saint is the self-serving arrogance that is the opposite of saintliness. One can only be a saint if one does not want to be a saint.

Same thing with getting into heaven—if you're trying to get into heaven, your motives must be highly suspect—you're only doing good for the reward, not the well-being of others. (Something I would have learned in 9th Grade if I had even read the Cliff's Notes for Jane Eyre.)

Whatever the motivation, kindness might be the one quality that saves humanity. True kindness is in limited supply in a world racked with violence and pain. So then my problem with do-gooders: Whatever their motivations, they do good works for their communities and the people who struggle to live in them. And yes, volunteers are the heart and soul of our ability to live in communities. Nevertheless, curmudgeon that I am slowly becoming, I'm always more intrigued—and awed—by those in our midst who do good when no one's keeping score. Helping someone with a door; allowing someone to merge into heavy traffic; a hand when you've tripped; seat on a train when you're pregnant or old or just beat. I like kindness that is not rewarded—or sometimes not even acknowledged.

The test for me regarding my own kindness—when I let people merge into traffic, do I get annoyed if they fail to acknowledge my good deed? If I do get annoyed, I'm not really being kind.

Enough philosophizing—remember Don Rumsfeld's unknown unknowns. And in a world where kids lives are scheduled from smart breakfasts through bedtime stories intended to increase their cognitive skills, where their upwardly immobilized parents put their fetuses names on pre-school lists and hire private tutors to write their kids college essays so they can get into Harvard and participate in the annually immoral Wall Street bonus parade, passing down a little bit of hippie philosophy might be the best thing we could do.

And where this is leading is the counter-intuitive question of spoiling the children.

Like most red-blooded, right-thinking Americans, you might have established it as an axiom of anti-establishment, anti-materiastic, anti-suburban life that it is wrong to spoil your kids—and even in the suburbs it is generally accepted as a reasonable approach to rearing responsible, moral, ethically sound children. But in this new age of aging, I've come around to thinking that it is not only a grandparental option but an imperative to spoil the grandkids unto eternal devotion. A duty.

Here is my illogic: Everyone on this earth should have the experience of knowing that there is someone or someones out there in the cold universe whose affection for you is pure and boundless. Someone(s) who are not bound to get you going on the right path in life, to mold you, shape you, bend you, scrape you (or "… compete with you, beat or cheat or mistreat you, classify you, simplify you, deny, defy, or crucify you"). So while it is natural that their parents are bound by nature and by law to teach them boundaries—as it should be—it is the grandparents' duty to acquaint them with the most basic principle of the universe—i.e., it is boundless.

So, please give up all those self-congratulatory liberal or conservative notions of restraint. In this instance, less is not more. That old cheapness-of-spirit Protestant work ethic should take the day off. Indulge your grandchildren to the outer limits of your own indulgence (and your income). And please keep in mind that indulgence doesn't have to be expensive—the medium is indeed the message.

So here are *The Chief's and Her Majesty's Nine Commandments*—who said there has to be ten?—*For Creative Spoiling of the Grandchildren*:

1. Always keep candy in your pocket. Need I explain? When your grandkids' parents say, "No more sweets, you're going to ruin your dinner," take the cute little pouters into another room and slip them a few life savers or gummi bears. By this point in life we know that a little candy is not going to ruin anybody's anything. Be smart, though; don't do it in front of the little buggers' parents and, in the interests of family harmony, restrain yourself from passing out said candy right before bedtime.

2. Whenever possible—except if you live next door to each other—bring the grandchild a present. Anything will do. Some crappy plastic toy. A crappy Golden book. A comic. A magazine. Support your local Dollar Store. My Aunt Miriam never showed up without some dime store piece of garbage, a little something from Woolworths. And when I had kids, she brought them little somethings from John's Bargain Stores. It was never really very much—and often something I never would have chosen—but those insignificant little presents always made me feel special—significant—in her life. Is there a better message than that for any child? And, of course, she holds a dear place in my memory for eternity.

3. Load up on cereals you wouldn't let your own kids eat. Save the Total and the Bran Flakes for your own intestinal health— when they come over, feed them Froot Loops and Lucky Charms.

4. Disregard all intentions to political correctness and tell each granddaughter, often and emphatically, that she is the most beautiful girl in the world.

5. As above, tell your grandson that he is the strongest boy in the world.

6. My father's favorite: Tell each grandchild that she or he is your favorite. The amazing thing is they all believe you. And when they find out many years later that you were not to be trusted, they don't care, remembering only how special they felt in your presence.

7. Let the grandchildren stay up past their bedtimes. (They won't last past eleven o'clock and, besides, they'll be going home in a day or two.)

8. Let them sleep in your bed if they want. (Or bribe them shamelessly if you don't want pointy elbows in your side or wet sheets underneath you.) It's your house and, as my daughter Clover taught us, nobody's the boss of you. You're not going to cause great emotional distress—or salvage their not-so-fragile psyches by making sure everyone gets a good night's rest.

9. Tell them there are more important things in life than homework. That serves at least two purposes: 1) It's true and all children need to know that they're not ruining the rest of their lives, like

teachers and parents are wont to suggest, just because they didn't do all the even problems on page 69. 2) It's a great way to irk your grown children, who spent years unto decades irking you by not doing their homework.

*

Look 'em over again: Nine simple gestures of boundless love. You will not only win the hearts of your grandchildren but, along the way, you will provide the one enduring life lesson that will rescue them from the abyss, wherever they find it: There are people on this earth whose wish to support you in everything you do is only exceeded by their unencumbered, unearned, unchanging love for you.

Chapter Nineteen

Empty Nest: Take One

Going down to Lonesome Town
—Ricky Nelson

---

*F*irst a quick memory exercise: remember "Grandma and Grandpa, my ass…."? [Hint: go back to Chapter 14]

Well, a little more than seven years and six grandchildren later, the story picks up as Patti and I, now officially known within the tribe as Damma and Chief, are moving Bay (child #6) into his dorm at East Carolina University. Once the bed is made with dark blue sheets (the better to not change them for an entire semester), the "discount" supplies charged at Target, the $525 of instantly-obsolete-edition textbooks purchased, the pointless questions asked and pointedly not answered, and the quiet tears shed all around, we slink into the blazing hot car and head back home with our "only child" Elizabeth.

Thus, after parenting seven kids over more than thirty-five years, Patti and I were at that moment within one child and less than two years from the famed Empty Nest Syndrome (ENS). From reports we've gathered from friends and family, all of whom emptied their nests long before we would, it was impossible to know whether it would be a cause for a glass of champagne or a dose of Prozac. Nevertheless, like overgrown (wrinkly) kids with their noses pressed to a fogged-up store window (a bakery? Christian Science Reading Room?), Patti and I certainly wondered from time to time just what an empty house would feel like.

After decades of sheer unadulterated chaos under this good roof, could empty nesting mean an endless series of quiet and romantic candlelit dinners...or just the two of us sitting at either end of a mile-long dining room table with barely enough hearing capacity left to hear each other? Would we find ENS to be leisurely Sunday mornings snuggling in bed, reading every section of the *Sunday Times* and sipping coffee from Tanzania...or crack o' dawn silent breakfasts of chopped cardboard and prunes and Sanka while reading large-print editions of last year's *Reader's Digest*?

Would we take spur-of-the-moment weekend jaunts to the Cape or down to Manhattan without a single worry about toddlers getting sick or teenagers trashing the house...or would we be sitting shoulder to shoulder in metal folding chairs by the front door, cordless phone in hand, waiting for a bell or a telephone ring...or just a measly postcard?

Well, that's pretty much the gist of what I was wondering as we drove home from Greenville. But no matter how I peered into the family crystal ball, with ENS already programmed on my internal global navigator, the vision of the two of us alone in this big country house unto eternity was, to use a regrettable phrase I probably uttered far too often after Cael was born in 1969, enough to blow my mind.

But apparently not enough to blow it sufficiently open to get ahead of the cosmic joke that greeted us upon arriving back in New Paltz: Nancy (#2), wearing a smile that reminded of the look on her face when she got another excellent report card from the Campus School, proudly announced that she and Michael and their two-year-old twin whirling dervishes were going to move in with us while their new house was being built down the road! Yeaaaaa!

Well, after I got my lower jaw back up where it's supposed to be—and the twins stopped looking like chimpanzees jumping up and down and squealing in delight—I calmly explained to myself over a medicinal pint of Guinness, that we were not yet officially empty nesters, and the twins really are very cute and very funny and very lovable and, best of all, when they throw their double-barreled tantrums (a hurricane-like force unknown to parents who raise kids one at a time), Patti and I, who are not their parents, could just get up and walk out of the newly crowded house.

Besides, with just a little mercy from the merciless gods of home construction, it actually turned out that a few months before we would officially become empty nesters, when Elizabeth was scheduled to fly the coop in 2006 (she did, see below), the twins actually had their own home to ransack (see below).

At least that was the plan. Or as much a plan as one could make in a family that is this many strong or loud or messy—and that was before Clover (#4) called from Boston to say that grandchild #21 was on the way! And then two months later Addie (#3) phoned with news of #22... and three months later, while Nancy, Mike, and the twins were living with us, we found out about #23.

Don't think for a minute that I'm complaining. I love the dizzying chaos that this family brings to my somewhat sensible life as much as anything on this good earth. But in the absence of any kind of original or creative thought that has been spun out of my spinning skull as our lives have circled in on themselves for more than three decades, I now understand that Patti and I have become the living embodiment of what some of you are saying right now to yourselves: *You made your bed and now you have a lot of people sleeping in it.*

Read on....

Empty Nest: Take Two Post-Post Partum

Do the chairs in your parlor seem empty and bare?
Is your heart filled with pain?
—The King

So yes, I've done the math more than once over the past thirty-eight years. The first time...I was a typical, unfocused, unkempt, unshaven, underachieving, and generally unrepentant sixth-year, anti-war undergraduate at the University of Wisconsin. Pacing across the messy living room of a drafty cottage on Lake Kegonsa with my brand-new colicky son howling into my shoulder, back and forth, back and forth, like someone afflicted with OCD, lips and fingers desperately trying to quantify how many years, months, days, minutes until the tiny screamer would be eighteen and I'd be my free-and-easy hipster self again.

Okay, so it was immature—and, of course, the arithmetic was premature at best. In the nineteen years that followed that July evening in 1969, as six more howling infants graced our sometimes graceless—and more often sleepless—lives, I calculated and re-calculated and re-calculated just how long it would be before that particular crying baby would fly the coop.

When I got bored or was overmatched by the confluence of math and calendar—which in my defense included leap years—I calculated simpler goals, like when the people-to-bathroom ratio would be less than two-to-one. Or when we could reasonably unload the VW van and buy a car like regular families. Or, as a measure of my most absurd delusions, the night when I would be able to drift off to sleep free from worry.

And, as long as I'm doing the math in such a public fashion, in those long evening hours of marital negotiation, before Elizabeth was conceived in 1987, six other children dreaming their own songs of freedom, I did the quick arithmetic and despaired at the thought that I would probably the oldest dad at high school graduation in 2006. I even checked some actuarial charts calculating, with a slight quiver of the lip, the odds of even making it to the Promised Land.

So now the family version of the Gene Tunney long-count is over. Elizabeth has indeed graduated from New Paltz High: trumpets, alarum, flourish, exeunt…we made it! Thirty-seven years, from "One more push, Babe" to Elizabeth shoving us out the door of her dorm room at Warren Wilson College in Asheville, North Carolina.

And to commemorate that oh-so-pregnant-with-meaning passage in life, our older kids, with a sweet lump of tongue-in-cheek, threw Patti and me a party celebrating the milestone: our "graduation" from the New Paltz Central School system. Thirty-two years from Cael's weepy entry into kindergarten to Elizabeth's white cap flying into the air.

As one might imagine, the party was heartening—so heartening!—our beautiful kids and dear friends all around. And predictably funny, too—graduation robes, mortarboards, a homemade "yearbook" of images documenting graduation by graduation their young parents' growing older—and then much older—than the teachers in the background. Sandwiched between the good food and the good drink, we happily endured the kinds of age-old jokes you might expect about "Super Seniors" and school colors being gray and gray, and questions about what college we were applying to…if only, of course, we could remember.

But, of course, it was a little disheartening. In this post-post partum world of long-anticipated empty nesting, Patti and I have found that there is also an overwhelming ache, a deep sadness in what has been lost through our newfound freedom. So there was no great sigh of relief, no Tiger Woods fist, in the air as we drove down the long rutted driveway back to our quiet house in the dark woods. Just a deep breath and, finally, some time for quiet reflection.

After all those kids and 32 years of stuffing ourselves in and out of skinny-chair desks at public school open houses, the rest of our lives out ahead in countless ways we never imagined, I think I finally understand something about the mathematics of life: the counting never stops. While *carpe diem* makes good copy, it's pointless advice, an ancient ruse perpetuated by dead poets and living self-help writers who profit from the fearful sound of "Time's winged chariot hurrying near."

In this vast post-Elizabeth universe I find that I'm listening more intently to the birds in our backyard, the coyotes howling just beyond the tree line; I hear more clearly the numerical buzz among the post-hippie crowd in post-hippie town: how long until retirement, 'til Medicare, how many "good" years we have left, the percentage of income one needs to live comfortably until the numbers cease to have meaning.

And with limits of time and the calculus of existence at my newly agile fingertips, this new wrinkle on the old counting has achieved a far more serious dimension. Free now to consider the world beyond my front porch, I am thinking exponentially, calculating numbers that will affect my grown children, their children and theirs—and theirs: the number of American deaths in Iraq since the beginning of the war—and counting; the massive federal government deficit—and counting; the average land surface temperature that has risen 0.45-0.6°C in the last century—and counting; sea level that has risen worldwide approximately 15-20 cm (6-8 inches) in the last century—and counting.

Today I count myself as angry as any grumpy old man when things just don't add up, as impatient as any young protestor demanding accountability, as mobilized and vocal as any toddler who knows the score.

I am sixty-one and it's the sixties all over again.

Day Four: Afterthoughts and Flashforwards

*"The '60s are gone, dope will never be as cheap, sex never as free,
and the rock and roll never as great"*
Abbie Hoffman

Paul Butterfield Blues Band
Everything's Gonna Be Alright
Driftin'
Born Under A Bad Sign
All My Love Comin' Through To You
Love March

Sha Na Na
Na Na Theme
Jakety Jak
Teen Angel
Jailhouse Rock
Wipe Out
Who Wrote The Book Of Love
Duke Of Earl
At The Hop
Na Na Theme

Jimi Hendrix
Message To Love
Getting My Heart Back Together Again
Spanish Castle Magic
Red House
Master Mind
Here Comes Your Lover Man
Foxy Lady
Beginning
Izabella
Gypsy Woman
Fire
Voodoo Child/Stepping Stone
Star Spangled Banner
Purple Haze
Woodstock Improvisation/Villanova Junction
Hey Joe

Chapter Twenty

Blood Simple

Why dont you all f-fade away (talkin bout my generation)
—The Who

I faked left and spun right, slicing past Michael to lay up a beautiful floater, an orange balloon drifting down through the sea breezy net and skidding off my aching feet. "Gotcha!" I snorted.

Michael shrugged and jogged off to join his wife, my daughter, on the beach.

This was back in the fall of 1998 and I still thought I was a menace on the basketball court. We were down on Hatteras Island, North Carolina, for our daughter Addie's wedding ... having just tied up the loose ribbons on her older sister Nancy's marriage to Michael that summer up here in the Hudson Valley. That's right, two weddings within 90 days. Born nineteen months apart, Nancy and Addie brought sibling rivalry to an living artform. One has never done anything that has not been construed as a direct challenge to the other, including getting hitched. The cost of two weddings ... well, don't get me started...but, frankly, money had little to do with the force that sent me driving to the hoop with such vengeance.

Mothers rejoice at their daughters finding true love. I was bereft in the way that fathers seem to concurrently age rapidly and grow more infantile when they receive news of a daughter's first period. Indeed, over the course of mostly getting in the way of my wife Patti's planning the two weddings, I was nothing less than clueless, ridiculous, cheap, sentimental, crotchety, and as adolescent as one grown man could be.

Of course, that last piece was the problem. Like too many men who came of age in the Sixties, I'm too much in touch with my inner teenager. Despite the sore knees. Despite the silvery hair and the crow's feet and, well, everything else that betrays my adolescent delusions. As Procol Harem once reminded a generation who found companionship in the bizarre notion of never trusting anyone over thirty, "… the mirror tells its tale."

And so it does. Six Thanksgivings after the twin weddings, with seven children, five spouses, a boyfriend, a girlfriend, and two granddaughters and four grandsons sitting shoulder to highchair to shoulder around the long (long) dining room table (and clogging up the garbage pails and septic field in our upstate New York home at an alarming rate), I felt as full as a man could be.

But if there's one thing I should have learned as a man with seven children and nine grandchildren, you can always squeeze in one more— or enough is not necessarily enough. So hey, I shouldn't have been surprised when daughter number three, Clover, announced that she was pregnant with her first child. It was wonderful news, of course.

You probably know where this is going…the sad thing is that I didn't. I was clueless. Having lived through decades of sibling rivalry and written widely (and perhaps wisely) about its natural evolution, I stunned when, two months later, Addie announced she was pregnant; then dumbstruck when, a few months after that, Nancy, with the twins clinging each to a leg, announced with frightened smirk that she, too, was pregnant! Actually, I was struck dumb, my lower lip trembling, my palms resting on my knees, like older players at the end of tough games.

Three babies in four months. I reflexively scanned the swirling house for the love of my life, but she wasn't anywhere in the picture. Someone somewhere, though, must have noticed the addled look on my face because I heard a lilting voice saying Patti was taking a walk in the woods.

Here's the thing: I'm not that old that I shouldn't have been sharp enough to be listening for the other sneaker to drop, as it always has with those two girls. However, I was probably still assuming that I had a few good moves left in me in case Elizabeth's boyfriend decided to challenge me to a game of one-on-one.

But Nancy's announcement put me right on the bench, tears and sweat plipping to the varnished hardwood of my dreams of immortality. Oh Lord, I groused in my unmistakeable joy and panic; I cannot stop this clock. I am not Lazarus. And I am certainly not Michael Jordan.

I am a grandfather. Ten times…now eleven times…and there's no end in sight. I may not be finished playing basketball or, as Bay and Elizabeth remind me daily, being a father, but I'm done trying to beat my daughters' men to the hoop. It's time to dish it off for real.

Time for all of us—especially all those sexagenarian rockers and the old guys and gals at vintage car shows—to stop playing the young person's game. Get off the stage. At this point in life we should have finally learned that there is real poetry and grace in the assist.

Chapter Twenty-One

To 'too or Not to 'too

> *"That is no country for old men"*
> —William Butler Yeats

"It's going to look like a scar!" my shocked wife exclaimed after I offered a sheepish one-word addendum to the meager one-word explanation of what was actually under the gauzy white bandage on my forearm.

"That is so cool!" my teenage son Bay blurted into the silence that had instantly chilled the warm kitchen.

Cael, my first-born son with two sons of his own, merely glanced at the anointed arm and shook his head at the overgrown teenager he sometimes ruefully calls Dad.

And so it went: A couple of days later a friend spied it at a faculty meeting and sputtered, "You are crazy!" Then a former student let it slip that she thought it was a blade of grass stuck to my forearm. But once and former beatnik Alan Goerlick (artist, salesman, golfer) brought it full-circle when we bumped into each other at the local Bakery: "It looks like a damn scar!" he snorted.

It is not a scar.

It's a three-inch tattoo of Hatteras Island. (FYI: Hatteras is a narrow barrier reef off the coast of North Carolina, and the thin black outline of the island shows a jagged left-hook right where you'd find the famous lighthouse … just like a scar. But, to repeat myself, which some say befits my age better than a tattoo, it is definitely not a scar.)

So what drives a moderately stable grandfather to drive up to Pat's

Tats on Rte 212 in legendary Woodstock, New York, for a young man's rutting ornament?

I'm tempted to just shrug my shoulders like one of my teenagers asked to explain why he missed curfew. But I'm not suggesting that I was Jimmy Buffet drunk on margaritas ... and I wasn't goaded on by a roving band of Huguenots whooping it up while the wives were out of town. I drove up to Woodstock alone (and sober) after teaching one Friday afternoon.

It stung considerably more than I imagined, though not nearly as much as I feared. And when the buzzing was done and the excess ink wiped away, the many-tatted Pat shook my hand and said my life would never be the same. That remains to be seen.

Of course I've suddenly had to learn to withstand with some grace all the smirking speculation in this psyche-conscious college town. Practically everyone who notices the "too" assumes it's just another mockable item in the well-laundered list of ways that middle-aged men attempt to colorize their fading virility. And I'd be an old fool, a "tattered coat upon a stick," as William Butler Yeats once wrote, to tell them they're wrong. They're right.

But this tattoo is more than a late, late late, middle-aged teenager's fantasy. It is also a talisman, a token, a cave drawing of paradise. It's much more about where I am going than where I'm coming from.

At sixty-one, I'm finding that life is far more complicated than I ever thought possible at forty-one—when I arrogantly figured I'd have the whole world right in the palm of my hand by the ripe old age of fifty-one. Over the past several years, fifteen new people, five spouses and ten babies, have been added to our already shoulder-crowded pine dining room table. And that's not counting Bay's Allison and Elizabeth's Kenny who might as well be part of this unwieldy clan. And the electric meter keeps cranking. And the gutters need cleaning. And my students keep writing papers. And the mailbox keeps coughing up bills. And the freelance deadlines don't drop dead. And the toilet doesn't stop running. And what is that noise in the basement? And when is that damn prostate exam? And just who is that kid on my couch?

A few summers ago Patti and I had to turn down three dinner invitations from some remarkably understanding neighbors because there was not an open Friday or Saturday in May, June, or July. And then, like kids barely escaping the clutches of the boogie man in the dark basement, we raced breathlessly off to the Outer Banks for our annual respite in August ... the Big Ahhhhhhhhhhhhhhhh.

It's not that I don't love life in this glorious funky upstate town ... the backwards river, the wild turkeys in the embraceable backyard, the utterly quirky life on Main Street. Or that we'll ever leave here. But Hatteras is a sanctuary, an island at the precarious edge of the Graveyard of the Atlantic that demands little and expects so much less.

On Hatteras, shoes are impediments and (personally speaking) underwear is an anathema. On my Hatteras, with its boxy beach cottages rising up on pilings, Monday at the Thrift Shop is the social event of the week. It is where the shrimp hauled off the trawlers out of Wanchese is 10 cents a piece at Hodad's and the fried mackerel dinner (baked beans, slaw, hush puppies, sweet tea) at the Rodanthe Community Center is $6. It is where the mosquito is the symbol for Debbie Bell's Rodanthe Surf Shop and the motto at Jobob's Trading Post is "If it's worth buying, we might have it."

Well, I think I have it, right here on my arm, as indelible as a scar. With this graven image right below the crook of my elbow, I have a vision of Byzantium. Now, whenever I run out of breath from this crazy life, all it takes is a quick turn of the wrist and I'm sailing off to Hatteras, the arc of azure sky and green water out beyond the breakers, the shifting shoals beneath my slowly treading feet.

Chapter Twenty-Two

My Resignation from the Old Men's Club

---

*T*he evolution of this final chapter provides an interesting and instructive turn of events. The initial plan was to gather suggestions about how to stay young and hip and relevant into one's dotage from high school and college students. After some initial discussions with smirking friends and some wiseass college kids, I thought this would be hysterical. My only concerns revolved around the young people taking themselves too seriously—and then what I'd be left with is the most tiresome of all prose: adolescent self-righteousness.

So I contacted various high school teachers and freshman comp instructors all over the country to request submissions from their students...expecting, as above, truly hysterical one-liners, bumper stickers, etc.....

The result? As of January 31, 2007, five months after I began the search, I got nothing. Nada. Nothing from a writer friend who teaches at the University òf Wisconsin. Nothing from a member of the writing faculty at Warren Wilson College in Asheville, North Carolina. Nothing from a former colleague teaching high school English in the Florida Keys. Nothing from a freshman comp instructor who teaches at Marist College and Ulster Community College. Nothing from two English teachers at New Paltz Central High School. Nothing.

Nothing.

Which was when I realized—V-8 slap on the expanding forehead—

that most young people don't even think about old people. We're invisible. (Need proof? Just take a stroll around a mall saying hello to as many teenagers as you can find and see how many answer you.) In fact, we're so far off their radar that even getting extra credit (as offered by Bill Zimmer to his high school English students) wasn't enough to motivate them to participate in this venture.

So it is for a generation that warned, then promised, to never trust anyone over thirty.

And then on February 1, 2007, having given in to the vast alienating silence of old age, I received a manila envelope in the mail from students in Michelle Diana' tenth grade Regents English class at New Paltz High School. And, as I've learned from these kids and others, beyond how to use a cell phone and a computer, listening is the key to staying hip. Listen up:

• Marissa Barrington wrote that "Most grandmas are old, boring, and they just love to tell you every time they see you about how their life was like when they were young." She goes on to say that "Fortunately, I have it different...(my grandma) is the coolest rocker I've known in my life."

• Bridget Kelly, in reflecting upon her grandmother, who "is not even clued into caller ID yet," recommends that older people overcome their fear of technology. She is giving her grandmother lessons on "how to use her 'too high tech' phone."

• Dan Rudder, in his essay on "The coolest, most hip older person I know," writes about a doctor he knows who "... does not hesitate to speak his mind.... He speaks of reality and of what really happens without hesitation."

• Ben Ramic writes about his uncle's ex-girlfriend Claire, who is "in her late sixties, and has recently gotten her second face lift...." She goes to clubs, wears Uggs and short skirts, and "... thinks it's *okay!*" Sometimes he thinks that "everybody should be as happy and fun as (she is)."

• Ksenia Konovalov lists several ways for older people to "Learn How to Fearlessly Approach the Teenagers of Today": 1) "Lecturing should be avoided at all costs." 2) "Teenagers don't have the attention span to listen to a whole recollection of their grandparents' lives." 3) "… asking teenagers about their lives is also very important." 4) "Being open-minded is the key to success … grandparents should let go of the past and grab a hold of the present and future."

• Jacob Crist recommends getting hip to the new technology: "Buy something that looks good, throw your manual away, flaunt that piece of technology, and you'll be sure to love Radio Shack just as much a ten-year-old boy."

• John Stephenson points to his dad as his "Favorite Old Guy." The "old guy" (forties? fifties?) is young at heart, isn't too strict, rarely preaches to him, and "knows that there is no point in telling stories that are gonna bore me."

• Amanda Cora wrote about her young-at-heart aunt who "… has the personality similar to a sophomore in college." She's a great listener, she "understands whatever position you are in…," has no "extra bulges," and "unlike some elderly people, understands the new technology."

• Gabriela O'Shea implores the older generation to "Embrace the electronic greatness!" She writes, "It's either learn or die resisting."

• Danielle Salinitri warns against "…people of the older generation pretending they are twenty-one, walking down Main Street wearing tight jeans, Uggs, an oversized purse and carrying a Starbucks drink."

• Robin Caskey, in an attempt to get her father to "dress like a more sophisticated, hip version of his fifty-year-old self," has advised him to wear "glasses that don't cover half his face" and never to wear white sneakers ("They're awful").

*

I'm thinking now of a Black Crowes concert I went to with my youngest daughter a few weeks before she left for college. (FYI, the Black Crowes are not synonymous with her generation or mine, but they had become deeply embedded in our family lore through her older brothers and sisters.)

And I'm remembering the twelve-year-old who sat behind us with his thirty-something parents who, in their old Crowes t-shirts and neatly creased jeans were movin' and groovin' to the beat. The kid, however, spent practically the entire concert with his head in his hands, hiding a scowl that went from jawbone to jawbone. It was if they had taken him to a Lawrence Welk concert.

Which reminded me of the pained looks on college kids' faces when compatriots from our generation begin talking about how loaded we were at Monterey or what a gas it was to live through such a creative, dynamic, explosive era (translation: The present sucks and your life is a paltry shadow of the good ol' days).

We have to stop it before it gets out of hand—before we start waxing on about 29 cents per gallon gas, 30 cents cigarettes, when a nickel was really a nickel bag. Recently I've been getting those FWD FWD FWD e-mails with graphics from the great products of our youth, like Swanson's TV Dinners and all that high-end TV we watched and, of course, how we spent our computerless/ipod-less youths using our imaginations (hanging out, siphoning gas, masturbating, dreaming).

Keep it to yourself. I don't even want to hear about it anymore.

*

And so, the final cautionary tale: So there I was just flipping through some family photo albums and wistfully recalling the old days in this funky upstate New York town, back in 1973, when we arrived from Wisconsin in a rusted Dodge van with two mop-headed little kids, a couple of cats, three dogs, and the hippie notion that we'd discovered Eden in a brick farmhouse with a red barn and a view of the mountain. And for a few moments it was heartwarming, if a little bittersweet, to see my then thirty-six-year-old son forever four and smiling in his Oshkosh overalls.

Then I turned to a faded 1974 Polaroid of me and an old friend, long-haired and long-departed, hamming it up in my old Chevy pickup. I think that was what started me grumbling about all the traffic in town.

Then carping about the rising taxes.

Then fretting about the savage hunger of developers eating away at our pastoral way of life.

I lamented that everything was changing, and for the worse.

Which was when my seventeen-year-old daughter Elizabeth, who had been draped on the arm of the couch looking at pictures with me, sighed and got up to walk away. I called her name, but when she turned, instead of that dazzling set of teeth I saw a scowl twist across her beautiful baby-smooth face.

I tilted my head like the family Springer Spaniel, trying to appear charmingly confused by her sudden change of countenance. But she kept walking and, frankly, I recognized that scowl instantly. It was the one I had worn more than forty years ago whenever my father and uncles got together.

It was always the same with them...the plaid-on-plaid foursome—Murray, Mac, Herman and my old man sitting around the den swapping stories about their glory days on the Lower East Side. Oh, I got an earful and a bellyful about the fabulous music of the twenties and thirties, the profound lessons of the Great Depression, the greatest president that ever lived, the greatest generation, a time when baseball was baseball and men were men...and then, somewhere after the cigars came out and the bottle of Johnnie Walker made its first turn, their chins receding into jowls, I'd hear the old rant about the country going into the gutter...the television, the rock 'n' roll, the protestors, the...well, fill in your own blanks. You were there.

That was always my cue to get up from the table with a scowl on my face and walk away. Just like Elizabeth.

After she disappeared from the room, I was left alone with my pictorial memories of the sixties and seventies, wondering just how and when I, devoted hipster that I am, had morphed into Uncle Mac. When exactly did I become a dues complaining member of the Old Man's Club?

Despite my long hair, poor fashion style, and continued devotion to a dead VW van in my barn, as a father of seven grown and growing children (and grandfather of eight), it was clear to all that I am old enough to be in the club. And I do have—and use to great advantage—my AARP card. And I have to admit that I was whining like an old pump.

But how did I end up volunteering for the 450th Cranky Division? I suppose there are as many reasons for it as there are rainy, achy days in our lives. Yet only having acted like a cranky old man for a couple of hours, I was already tired of this club and our pointless complaints about computers and television and skateboards and hats worn backwards and pants slung too low and rude, lazy, ignorant, unpolitical and arrogant teenagers.

So, neophyte that I am, I am submitting herewith my official resignation from the Upstate New York chapter of the Old Man's Club. I quit. Frankly, I don't know what other club will have me, but I'm not going back to Crankytown.

In following the trail of crumbs around the house to find Elizabeth (and to yell at her for dropping crumbs) and apologize for my miserable behavior, I realized that the worst legacy we could leave the next generation is not the intrepid advances of a universe that grows and changes in spite of itself, but it is to tell our children and grandchildren—as we were all told—the big lie that change is bad.

And as a form of penance for my poor attitude, there is this book: With this book I am embracing the Sixties, the old one and the new one, laughing joyfully at where we've been and grooving on all the possibilities that lie out ahead of us.

It has been one helluva long and strange trip from the infamous Sixties. With a little help from our friends, I'm hoping that the second sixties will be even stranger.

About the Author

Patti and Steven Lewis nearing their second Sixties.

Steven Lewis is a longtime mentor at SUNY-Empire State College, an instructor at the Sarah Lawrence College Writing Institute, father of seven and grandfather of ten (and counting). His credits include *The New York Times Magazine, Washington Post, Los Angeles Times, New York Times, AARP Magazine, Ladies Home Journal,* and *The Christian Science Monitor.* Previous books include *Zen and the Art of Fatherhood; The ABC's of Real Family Values;* and *The Complete Guide for the Anxious Groom.*